PRAISE FOR

the prayer dare

Prayer means having a living conversation with the God of the universe, who in Christ calls us "friend." This places prayer at the core of our adventure of listening to and following Jesus Christ. *The Prayer Dare* is Ron Kincaid's encouragement to take the risk of stepping into that adventure with confident and humble hope and faith.

MARK LABBERTON
Lloyd John Ogilvie Associate Professor of Preaching
Fuller Seminary School of Theology

Our family has known Ron Kincaid for many years. On many occasions during committee meetings and other encounters in responsible situations, Ron has led in prayer. You can instantly tell that he lives it not as a theory but as an experience. He lives in the presence of God and ministers the Word of God with authority because of it. Look at the title of this book and you will recognize that he deeply knows what it is to walk with God in prayer. It will also excite you to pick up whatever chapter suits your situation at the moment. You will be blessed!

LUIS PALAU
World Evangelist
Luis Palau Association

The impressive thing about this book is that the author practices what he preaches. As a member of his church, I know Ron to be a person of prayer in every way. Many have been amazed by Ron's uncanny ability to remember the names of so many people in his church. What they don't know is that he regularly prays for them by name. Ron knows firsthand the power of prayer, and I believe that anyone reading this book will develop a deeper appreciation for prayer as well.

JOHN FRANKLIN
Young Life Western Division Senior Vice President
Portland, Oregon

We have enough books that teach us *about* prayer. In *The Prayer Dare*, Ron Kincaid helps us pray with a tool that is practical and revitalizing. I know of no one more qualified to offer the church such a gift. Ron is one of the most faithfully prayerful men I know, and his life and ministry are a fruitful reflection of that discipline.

MARK TOONE
Pastor, Chapel Hill Presbyterian Church
Gig Harbor, Washington

RON KINCAID

the prayer dare

TAKE THE
CHALLENGE
THAT WILL
TRANSFORM
YOUR
RELATIONSHIP
WITH GOD

Revell

a division of Baker Publishing Group
Grand Rapids, Michigan

© 2010 by Ron Kincaid

Published by Revell
a division of Baker Publishing Group
PO Box 6287, Grand Rapids, MI 49516-6287
www.revellbooks.com

Revell edition published 2015
ISBN 978-0-8007-2533-4

Previously published by Regal Books

Printed in the United States of America

Library of Congress Control Number: 2015948681

To my mother, Dorothy.

Thank you, Mom, for leading me to Christ and setting an example
for me of the importance of prayer. I remember as a young boy knocking
on your bedroom door or sometimes just barging in to find you on your
knees beside the bed praying. You had various papers spread out before you
on the bed with prayer requests. You were a Bible Study Fellowship teaching
leader, and you were praying for your leaders and the members of their
groups. You were also praying for Dad, my sister and me.

You continued to pray for me when I became a Young Life leader and
when I became a pastor. You have prayed faithfully for Jorie and me.
You have also prayed for our nine children. You have prayed for Jorie and
me, as we have given our lives to full-time ministry. You spend hours each
day in prayer. I am certain that much of the spiritual fruit God has
granted to Jorie and me has come as a result of your prayers.

Thank you for being a woman of prayer.

To my wife, Jorie.

We first prayed together when we worked together as Young Life
leaders at Deerfield High School in Illinois. You became my head girl leader
in a ministry that God blessed immensely. Scores of high school students
gave their lives to Christ during those exciting years, and many of them are
continuing to make a difference for Christ today. I am certain that much
of the fruit was the result of your prayers.

Then as we began to date, I greatly enjoyed praying with you. Your
strong faith in Christ was an inspiration to me. I always felt more confident
that God had heard our prayers after praying with you.

Then when we got married and I was called to pastor a church,
I came to rely heavily on our times of prayer together. You have taught me
the importance of praise. It is not uncommon for the first 15 to 20 minutes
of our prayer time together to be nothing but praise. By the time we praise
God for who He is and what He is doing, I am certain that God can handle
any problems we are facing.

We constantly pray together for our kids. As we added children to our
family, our prayer times became longer. I am always encouraged by your deep
faith in God as we pray. By the time we are done praying, I have renewed
confidence that God will bring all things together for good for our children.

Thank you for being a woman of prayer.

CONTENTS

It probably goes without saying that if we want God to answer our prayers, we must pray. God could probably meet all our needs without us praying, but the Bible is clear that He wants us to ask. God insists that we pray, because He knows that when we ask, we will be more likely to give Him the glory.

A well-known business axiom states, "If you want to know something, ask an expert." It makes sense, then, that if we want to learn how to pray, we should go to the expert on prayer. So we will go to Jesus, for there's no One better to instruct us in prayer.

If a tired neighbor gives us what we need, how much more will God, who never sleeps, give us all that we need? Jesus says that we should pray boldly and constantly, because God is more than willing to answer and meet our needs.

We have to truly understand how much God loves us. When we pray to God, He will not give us things that are bad for us. He only gives us good gifts.

A Challenge from the Author

I challenge you to commit to praying for a set amount of time, and I invite you to pray like you have never prayed before. I dare you to enter into a deeper relationship with God through prayer.

This challenge is not to be entered into casually, but I know—from personal experience—that this is a challenge that *can* be met.

I believe I'm qualified to issue this challenge because not only have I been a committed pray-er for all my Christian life, but I also have direct evidence—in the form of a 30-year-long prayer journal in which I've recorded over 40,000 answers to specific requests I have made of God—that when one commits to praying, God shows up.

What started as a personal record has turned into an incredible logbook of God's faithfulness. Some of the prayers I've uttered—whether on my own behalf, the lives of others, the Church or the world—have returned astonishing answers. Some answers have come right away, while others have taken years. I've learned a lot over the past 30 years, but perhaps one of the most astounding things I've learned is how powerful *the act of committing to prayer* is. I've also learned that when prayers are offered in the right way with the right motives and with the right approach, God delivers answers.

Try it. Read this book and learn. Humble yourselves for 40 days. See if your life—and the lives of others—changes in ways you'd never, ever expect.

If you'd like to commit to this on your own, by all means, do so. If you feel led to enter into this with a spouse, a friend, your family, your small group at church or perhaps a whole congregation, accept my challenge that way. Once committed, grab your calendar and choose a length of time that you believe you can stick with. (I suggest at least 40 days, though you could certainly extend this to two months or a year.)

However you choose to try it, keep in mind that this adventure is not designed for dabbling. Those who stop partway through will miss out on the greatest benefits. But if you stick with it to the end, it will change your life.

What are you waiting for? Go ahead.

I dare you.

Ron Kincaid

Introduction

After graduating from college, I drove east where I enrolled in divinity school. While there, I was asked to start and lead a Young Life club for some high school students. I was invited to meet the young people at a barbecue, where I was introduced as the new Young Life leader. Twenty students showed up: 18 girls and 2 guys. When I went home that night, I thought to myself, *What a disaster! I can't start a Young Life club when I only know two guys.* In my experience, girls will come if the guys are there, but it doesn't usually work the other way around. It seemed to me that I needed to know at least 50 guys before announcing the first Young Life club meeting.

Although I had been a Christian since I was eight years old and had the privilege of growing up in a strong Christian home, leading a Young Life club was a big challenge for my faith. The prospect of meeting high school students, writing talks every week, and inviting kids and their parents to grow in faith sent me to my knees. I knew I could not reach students for Christ and build a Young Life club. Only God could do that. So I prayed for God to show His power and grace, and I prayed for God to help me meet 48 more guys from the high school before starting the club.

The Monday after the barbecue I headed to the high school during the lunch hour to meet some kids, particularly guys. I had a small problem, however: The two guys I knew would not be easy to find in this school of 2,600 students. So I prayed for God to please help me find Mike O'Shea or Mark Hogan, the two guys I had met at the barbecue. As I opened the door to the school, there was only one student walking down the long corridor: Mike O'Shea. Mike was just heading to lunch, and he introduced me to tons of his friends.

As I left the school that day, I praised God for leading me to Mike O'Shea at the high school. What were the chances that out of 2,600 students, the only one walking down the hall as I walked in was Mike O'Shea? I knew it was no coincidence. God had answered my prayer.

That was just the start of many amazing ways God has answered my prayers. Some of the answers to my prayers have seemed even more unbelievable—so much so that I thought no one would believe me, so I started keeping a prayer journal in which I recorded answers to specific requests I made of God.

Now, after leading two Young Life clubs and serving as a pastor for 30 years, I am still keeping a prayer journal. (At this point, I have recorded over 40,000 answers to specific requests I have made of God.) This book is about getting you started on your own journey with prayer. It is an invitation for you to discover a deeper and more vital relationship with God through prayer. It is an invitation for you to grow in confidence in prayer. I would like you to experience the love and power of God by seeing God answer your prayers.

Each chapter of this adventure includes these four important elements:

1. *A real-life experience involving prayer.* First, I will share an example of how God answered a prayer in my life or the life of another person (often someone in the

Bible), or I will tell a true story that illustrates some aspect of prayer. My hope is that my examples and illustrations will help you learn more about prayer and how to pray more effectively.

2. *Scripture about prayer.* Second, we will look at a Scripture verse and/or a story in the Bible to see what God teaches us about prayer.

3. *Space to answer questions.* Next, you will have space to answer questions that get you to focus on a particular aspect of prayer. Answering these questions will better prepare you for the challenge I'll give you.

4. *A prayer dare.* Finally, you will be given a challenge to pray in a specific way. I hope that as you go through this book, you will be able to build on what you learned the time before so you will feel as if you are growing in your understanding and practice of prayer. It's likely that on some days, you may not feel as if you fulfilled the prayer dare. But don't give up. Push on to the next dare.

Most of us have an idea that prayer is important. Most of have a sense that we ought to pray more, but we may not feel like we know how to pray. This book is an attempt to fill in that gap, to give you practical experience in prayer so that you grow in confidence in prayer and make it part of your life.

1

You Have to Ask

You want something but don't get it. You kill and covet,
but you cannot have what you want. You quarrel and fight.
You do not have, because you do not ask God.
JAMES 4:2

The last half of 2005 was wild for me. On September 9, 2005, I received a phone call at 5:00 A.M. from my son Luke. He was in Kenya with my wife, Jorie, preparing for a mission trip of 62 people from our church going to serve in Kenya. He said, "We've been in a really bad car accident. Our car flew off the road and hit a tree, and Mom's hurt badly. She broke her back! We need you to call the insurance to get permission for her to be life-flighted to the Nairobi Hospital." In the few minutes we had to talk, I learned she could have easily been killed and it was a miracle she wasn't paralyzed.

I went right to work so that she could be flown to a hospital where she could get the help she desperately needed. As it turned out, I spent a lot of time on the phone the next two weeks, talking to doctors and insurance people to get Jorie critical medical attention and to get her home. Once she got home, I spent hours driving her to doctors and taking care of her. I gained a whole new respect for all she did around the house and with the kids, as that responsibility had shifted to me. Carrying on with my usual duties of leading the church and preparing messages, I found I had a lot less time for things I used to do. One thing I skimped on was my prayer time.

Why when we are busy are we prone to cut short our prayers? Why are we so quick to stop praying when we have so much to do? During those stressful months, I needed to pray all the more for Jorie to be healed. I needed to pray for our kids to thrive, even though they had the misfortune of having me in charge (everyone in our family knows I can't cook and that I'm not as fun and easygoing as Jorie). I needed to pray all the more for our church during this time when I faced greater challenges at home. When I was so extra busy, I needed to pray more, not less. As Martin Luther said, "I have so much to do that I shall spend the first three hours in prayer."

God loves us, and He wants to meet our needs. God wants to intervene in our lives and help us achieve what we want. But He insists that we ask. "You want something but don't get it. You kill and covet, but you cannot have what you want. You quarrel and fight. You do not have, because you do not ask God" (Jas. 4:2).

In John Bunyan's classic *Pilgrim's Progress,* Christiana and Mercy learn that God often does not meet our needs because we fail to ask:

> Christiana and Mercy saw they would not be able to get safely away from two rude boys, so they both cried out for help; and as they were not very far from the gate, Goodwill heard them, and sent a man at once to see what had happened.
>
> The man ran quickly, and soon overtook the children. As he drew near, he called to the boys, saying, "What are you doing? How is it that you dare to hinder the

King's pilgrims?" When the boys heard the man's voice, they let Christiana and Mercy go free, and hurried to the wall. They climbed it as fast as they could, and dropped over into the Wicked Prince's garden. The children were very glad to see them disappear, and Christiana began to thank the man for his kindness in coming to help them.

"You need not thank me," he said, "but it is not good for little girls to travel alone. I was surprised that you did not ask Goodwill to send a guide with you. Your brothers are not old enough to be of much use."

"We never thought about the danger" said Christiana, "or that we should need a guide. I wish we had asked for one! Why did not Goodwill send someone with us if he knew that it was not safe for us to be alone?"

"The King does not allow him to send guides unless the pilgrims wish for them," replied the man.

God won't force His assistance on us. We must ask for His help. Why? Why should we pray when God already knows everything? He knows what we need before we ask. So why ask? God insists that we ask because He wants us to learn to depend on Him and give Him the credit for intervening in our lives. He knows that we won't give Him the credit unless we ask. God could probably have healed Jorie, blessed our children and taken care of the church without me praying, but the Bible makes clear that God wants us to ask.

Why do we find it so hard to ask? Why are we prone to cut short our prayers? Religious pollster George Barna reported recently that out of 12 priorities, pastors ranked prayer dead last, with only 3 percent ranking prayer as their top priority. The average pastor spends only 10 minutes a day in prayer.[1]

These are pastors! We can only imagine how the rest of the Body of Christ does.

Howard Hendricks once spoke to 175 couples and asked them to be honest as they wrote down whether they prayed regularly with their spouse. Only 17 (about 10 percent) said they prayed regularly with their spouse.

Why do we skimp on our prayers? Busyness? Laziness? Apathy? The reason I am writing this book is to inspire you to pray. I want you to experience the amazing power in prayer and show you how you can pray more effectively. So, to start off, learn the first principle of prayer: Pray. We can't have our prayers answered if we don't pray and ask first.

THE DARE

The first part of this dare is fairly straightforward. You have to pray. Prayer isn't just something you do when you are in church or before you dive into dinner. It is an ongoing conversation you have with God throughout the day.

First, write "You have to pray!" on several stick-on notes or scraps of paper. The idea is to stick or tape them to your alarm clock, mirrors, car visor, cell phone, refrigerator, computer monitor, lamps, front door and other such places to remind you to talk to God about everything in your day. Go ahead. Find a pen.

Next, take a few moments to think through and answer the following questions based on this chapter.

_____

_____

_____

_____

What happens if we don't pray?

_____

_____

_____

_____

_____

Why does God choose to work in response to our prayers?

_____

_____

_____

_____

_____

What are a few things that you want to commit to pray about before moving on to the next chapter?

_____

_____

_____

_____

_____

Note

1. The Barna Group, "Church Priorities for 2005 Vary Considerably," February 14, 2005. http://www.barna.org/barna-update/article/5-barna-update/185-church-priorities-for-2005-vary-considerably?q=gender+differences.

2

Know the One to Whom You Are Praying

One day Jesus was praying in a certain place.
When he finished, one of his disciples said to him, "Lord, teach us
to pray, just as John taught his disciples."

LUKE 11:1

A well-known business axiom states, "If you want to know something, ask an expert." If you want to know about golf, ask Phil Mickelson. If you want to learn how to play tennis, talk to Roger Federer. If you want to improve in basketball, go to Kobe Bryant. If you want to improve in swimming, see Michael Phelps. If you're interested in movies, approach Steven Spielberg. If you want to know the latest about computers, side up to Bill Gates.

It makes sense, then, if you want to learn how to pray, to go to the expert on prayer. And the greatest authority on prayer is Jesus Christ.

Jesus had a whole planet of people to save in a just few short years. So if anyone was busy, it was Jesus. Yet the Gospels tell us that Jesus frequently paused from His busy schedule in order to pray.

Prayer was more important to Jesus than food. We read that Jesus often got up long before breakfast: "Very early in the morning, while it was still dark, [Jesus] left the house and went off to a solitary place, where he prayed" (Mark 1:35).

Prayer was more important to Jesus than gathering large crowds. The Bible says, "News about [Jesus] spread all the more, so that crowds of people came to hear him and to be healed of their sicknesses. But Jesus often withdrew to lonely places and prayed" (Luke 5:15-16).

Prayer was more important to Jesus than sleep. The Bible says, "One of those days Jesus went out to a mountainside to pray, and spent the night praying to God. When morning came, he called his disciples to him and chose twelve of them" (Luke 6:12-13). Before His trial and crucifixion, He prayed long into the night (see Mark 14:32-41).

Prayer was more important to Jesus than celebrating great victories. After feeding the 5,000, when the people were so excited that they wanted to make Him king, "He dismissed the crowd. After leaving them, he went up on a mountainside to pray" (Mark 6:45).

Why was prayer so important to Jesus? What did He know about prayer that apparently we do not? What did Jesus know about prayer that apparently even His disciples didn't know? The disciples had observed how much Jesus prayed. They had seen all the amazing miracles He performed. They had figured out that Jesus was connected to God's power through prayer. So they said to Him to teach them: "One day Jesus was praying in a certain place. When he finished, one of his disciples said to him, 'Lord, teach us to pray, just as John taught his disciples'" (Luke 11:1).

You can almost hear them: "Lord, how come prayer is so important to you? You're the Messiah. You're the Son of God. If you need to pray, we need to pray all the more. When we pray, we can't think what to say after a few minutes, but you pray through the night. We yawn and grow sleepy when we pray, but you stay alert for hours. What's your secret?" Jesus knew that prayer was critical to developing an intimate relationship with God; in fact, He had such a close relationship with His Father that He prayed about everything. And He knew that prayer is how to tap into God's power.

So Jesus told the disciples to start praying by remembering to whom they are praying. Bear in mind that this is no small deal. This is the Son of God telling how to pray. He said to them, "When you pray, say: 'Father, hallowed be your name'" (Luke 11:2). In the parallel text in Matthew, Jesus said, "Our Father in heaven" (Matt. 6:9). The point Jesus made is that any pray-er must recognize and acknowledge the One to whom the prayer is addressed: You are praying to your *Father in heaven*. To address God as your Father is to recognize that He loves you like a father. As a father, He delights when we bring our requests to Him.

But God is not just any father. He is your Father in heaven. He is the Creator of the universe, who resides in heaven. To mention that your Father resides in heaven reminds you that your loving Father is also the all-powerful Creator of the universe. When you begin your prayers, Jesus wants you to remember that you will be speaking to a Father who loves you and who has the power to deal with any problem you face.

Jesus' words remind me of the way David ended Psalm 62: "One thing God has spoken, two things have I heard: that you, O God, are strong, and that you, O Lord, are loving" (Ps. 62:11-12). When you remember that God is strong and loving, you know that what His love directs, His power is able to perform. There is nothing too great for His power and nothing too small for His love.

THE DARE

Today's dare is to tell God every time you pray that you recognize He is your Father in heaven and that He is loving and strong. It will help you put your heart into your prayers by remembering to whom you are praying. Start out by actually saying, "My Father in heaven." Remind yourself that He loves you and is fully able to meet your needs. Next, think about and answer the following questions.

Do you really believe that God loves you? Why or why not?

_____

_____

_____

_____

_____

How strong is God? Do you really believe that He is more than a match for any situation you face?

_____

_____

_____

_____

_____

3

Understand that God Is Willing

[Jesus said,] I tell you, though he will not get up and give him the bread because he is his friend, yet because of the man's boldness he will get up and give him as much as he needs.

LUKE 11:8

After Jesus taught the disciples what to pray, He told them a parable: "Suppose one of you has a friend, and he goes to him at midnight and says, 'Friend, lend me three loaves of bread, because a friend of mine on a journey has come to me, and I have nothing to set before him'" (Luke 11:5-6).

Now, you have to imagine what things were like in Bible times. In Jesus' day, a typical house consisted of one room where the family would spend the day and a loft where the parents and children would sleep at night. At night the animals were often brought inside to bed down on the lower living area. Now imagine that late one night, well after a man and his family had gone to bed, someone knocks at the door. The man gets up out of bed, winds his way through the children, climbs down the loft ladder, pushes his way through the animals, and wakes the entire house with the clanging commotion he makes as he removes the large crossbar from the door. A friend from out of town stands at the entry. He needs a place to stay and he's hungry. What to do but invite him in and feed him. It would be rude to do otherwise.

Our host, however, is aghast to find that he has no bread. What can he do? He decides that his neighbor, a friend of his, will help. Of course, the neighbor and his family and their animals also are asleep. The man knows what an imposition bothering the neighbor will be, but he has no choice. He must give his guest something to eat.

The scene shifts to the neighbor's house, where the man naturally finds the door shut and locked. He knows it would be discourteous to knock on the door unless it was imperative, so he knocks.

Then there's a long silence. It seems like a lifetime before there's a response. The neighbor is angry. "Who's there?" he yells from his bed. "What do you want at this hour?"

"Friend, lend me three loaves, for a traveler has come and I have nothing to feed him." He waits. Then he hears the friend say, "Don't bother me. The door is already locked, and my children are with me in bed. I can't get up and give you anything" (Luke 11:7). He probably turns over in bed, determined to go back to sleep. But the children are now wide awake. The chickens and goats stir. The dog begins to bark. Again the persistent knocking. Finally, there is no alternative but to get up and give the man the bread he needs.

Jesus explained that "though [the neighbor] will not get up and give him the bread because he is his friend, yet because of the man's boldness he will get up and give him as much as he needs" (Luke 11:8).

Some people miss the meaning of this parable. Their thinking goes something like this: The neighbor did not want to get up and help, but because his friend was persistent in asking, he finally got him the food he needed. Likewise, we must persist in prayer, and God will give us what we ask. The problem with this interpretation is that there is no surprise in the parable. In every parable of Jesus, we find an element of surprise, and it is at the moment of surprise that we find the main point of the parable.

To grapple with this parable, we must understand Middle Eastern hospitality. In a Semitic village, a traveler is an honored guest. To not offer food would be a terrible breach of etiquette. When Jesus described a sleeping neighbor not wanting to help, his listeners would have been horrified to hear the neighbor say, "Don't bother me. I'm already asleep," for no member of the village would think of refusing to help a guest. Such a refusal would be an insult to the whole town. The surprise of the parable is that the man considered not getting up to help his neighbor serve a traveler. No one could imagine such a thing happening.

Jesus did go on to say that even if the neighbor wouldn't get up because of mutual friendship, he *would* get up and give his friend all he needs so that he would not lose face before the entire village. Jesus' conclusion then moves from the lesser to the greater: If a tired neighbor gives you what you need, how much more will God, who never sleeps, give you? Jesus said that just as He prayed constantly and persistently, so should you pray, because God is more than willing to meet your needs.

THE DARE

Last time, I asked you to tell God every time you pray that you recognize He is your Father in heaven and that He is loving and strong. Now I want you to continue this practice, but I also want you to remember that you pray to a God who is more than willing to meet your needs. You don't need to be afraid. Like the friend at midnight, don't hesitate to bring your needs to God.

Today's dare is to tell God that you're not afraid to bring your needs to Him, because you know that He is more than willing to meet those needs. He is willing to help, if you will just ask. Feel free to write your prayer below.

_____

_____

_____

_____

_____

Is there some request you've been hesitant to ask of God? Write that request here. (If it will help, knock on a door or wall and then present your request to God.)

_____

_____

_____

_____

Does knowing the fact that God is more than willing to meet your needs give you more confidence to pray?

_____

_____

_____

_____

_____

Have you started a prayer journal yet? If not, start one now and record the prayer requests you have already made. Also record in your journal any answers to your prayers. Or you can record the answers on a letter-sized sheet of paper, and after the paper is filled, drop it in a file folder labeled "answers to prayer."

4

Praying When You Fear that God Won't Give the Answer You Want

Which of you, if his son asks for bread, will give him a stone? Or if he asks for a fish, will give him a snake? If you, then, though you are evil, know how to give good gifts to your children, how much more will your Father in heaven give good gifts to those who ask him!
MATTHEW 7:9-11

The day I really came to grips with these verses in Matthew, which are nearly identical to Luke's account in Luke 11:11-12, was a turning point in my life when it comes to prayer. The summer after graduating from college, I began dating a girl in Portland. We had a wonderful summer working together with high school and college students in the church where I worked. Things were going well in our relationship and had they progressed, I presume we would have discussed marriage. When the fall came, I headed off for graduate school in Chicago, but I came back to visit her for Christmas. We had a wonderful few days together. On the last night, after we had exchanged our Christmas gifts, to my surprise she suggested we needed to put the brakes on our relationship. Of course I said, "All right." But I assumed that she wanted to tap the brakes gently, just to slow the speeding love train down a bit. I soon learned, however, that her intent was to slam down hard on the brakes and move to another set of tracks.

As a result, I was thoroughly depressed when I went back to Chicago for my second term of seminary. Every day I prayed for God to change my girlfriend's mind and help us get back together. After a number of weeks of melancholy pleading with God the same way every day, one day I got on my knees and prayed in a different way. I quoted Jesus' words in Matthew 7:9-11. I said, "God, I know that if I ask you for bread, you will not give me a stone. I know if I ask you for a fish, you will not give me a snake. I know you love me and only give me good gifts. I have asked for you to help me get back with my girlfriend. Since that does not seem to be happening, and you only give good gifts, it must mean that you must have somebody *better* for me. I'm sad, but I believe your promise that you only give good gifts, so I want you to know that I'm ready for you to bring another girl who is even better for me into my life. Or, if you don't have somebody for me, I am willing to go it alone." Once I said that prayer, the depression that had hung over me like the morning fog was suddenly lifted. I felt like a new man. My spirit was lighter. I trusted God was looking out for me.

A couple months later God brought Jorie (who would soon become my wife) into my life. She is a godly, beautiful, intelligent and talented woman; and she's far better suited for me than the other gal would have been. She has been an unbelievably good gift to me. God heard my cry and was happy to meet my need.

Do you understand that God hears your cries as well? He knows the anxiety you feel over an impending surgery, the exasperation you feel over a difficult son or daughter, the desperation you feel over your marriage, the struggle you face in caring for an aging parent, or your heartfelt desire to find a dating or marriage partner.

You must truly understand how much God loves us. We tend to think that God is like the neighbor, quite reluctant to give us what we ask for. Martin Luther said, "Prayer is not overcoming God's reluctance, but laying hold of his willingness." Our problem is that we may not pray because we fear that God won't give us the answer we want. What we fail to understand is that God loves us so much that He is willing and eager to give us the good gifts He has in store for us.

As a pastor, I have been called late at night to counsel people who are suicidal, help families in a domestic crisis or visit those who have been suddenly hospitalized. One time a woman called me after midnight because her husband had just had a serious heart attack. My first thought was to go back to sleep and visit them first thing in the morning. Jorie stuck her toe under the covers into my thigh and said, "Come on, get dressed. Get going!"

We tend to think that God is as reluctant to help as we are, but He is not.

THE DARE

Maybe there is something that has happened in your life that grieves you. It makes you sad. Possibly you wonder why God allowed it to happen to you.

Today's dare is based on Matthew 7:9-11. Read this passage of Scripture, and then try repeating the verses as you pray. Tell God that you believe He only gives good gifts. If He took something away from you, it can only mean that He has something better for you. Tell God today that you are going to stop resenting what has happened and start trusting that He has good things in store for you. You are going to quit feeling sorry for yourself and start believing that God only gives good gifts.

Write out your prayer. It may be a turning point in your life.

_____

_____

_____

_____

_____

_____

Now, write down how trusting that God only gives good gifts gives you a new perspective on things that have happened in your life.

_____

_____

_____

_____

_____

_____

5

Don't Give Up

Ask and it will be given to you; seek and you will find; knock and the
door will be opened to you. For everyone who asks receives;
he who seeks finds; and to him who knocks, the door will be opened.
LUKE 11:9-10

I asked a co-worker to help me with something once. She said
she would come down when she had a minute. She never came.
I asked her another time to help me with something and she
did, but she made me feel as if my request was a real imposition. So I stopped asking her for help.

We're all like that. We ask for help once or twice, maybe
three times; but if we either don't get a response or if the response is negative, we stop asking. In behavioral science jargon,
our motivation is extinguished.

We're not to think that way, though, when it comes to praying to God. Jesus said we are to ask, seek and knock. All three of
those words—"ask," "seek" and "knock"—in the original Greek
are in the present tense, which means we are to keep on asking,
keep on seeking and keep on knocking. We're not to stop. Just because our prayer is not answered the first time or the second time
or the third time . . . or the tenth time, we're to keep on asking.

If you're like most people, you give up on your prayers far
too quickly. George Müller, the English orphanage director
who was known for his prayers, wrote:

The great point is to never give up until the answer comes. I have been praying every day for 52 years for two men, sons of a friend of my youth. They are not converted yet, but they will be! The great fault of the children of God is that they do not continue in prayer. They do not go on praying; they do not persevere. If they desire anything for God's glory, they should pray until they get it.[1]

One of these men became a Christian at Müller's funeral, the other some years later. So Müller's prayers were not answered until after he died!

As I told you at the beginning of this book, I have kept a prayer journal for 30 years. In this journal, I write answers to prayer. I also keep a list of people I am praying for. I pray for my family. I pray for my church staff and their families. I pray for the elders in my church and their families. I also keep a list of people I know who I do not believe have put their trust in Christ. They are people God has put in my life who, as far as I know, do not know Christ. I pray for them at least once a week, that the Holy Spirit would draw them to Christ and that I might have opportunities to build my relationship with them and some day share Christ with them. Some of them have shown an interest in learning about Christ and others are far from faith and don't want to hear anything about Jesus. Nevertheless, I pray for all of them every week. Some of them have been on my list for years. Just because they don't seem eager to talk about Christ or don't seem interested in coming to church is no reason for me to give up on them. I keep on praying for them. I'm not giving up on them until God does.

Jesus ended the parable about a man asking his neighbor for help by saying that we should *keep on asking; keep on seeking*

and we will find; keep on knocking and the door will be opened to us. For every one who keeps on asking, receives; everyone who keeps on seeking, finds; and everyone who keeps on knocking, will find the door opening (see Luke 11:9-10). In other words, Jesus said to keep praying. Continue to ask until you receive. Even if you don't receive answers right away, keep on asking, because God loves you and will meet your needs when the time is right.

THE DARE

For today's dare, I would like you to write down some requests that you've stopped praying for that you need to get back to praying for. It might be changes in your life that need to be made. It might be people you need to pray for that God wants to be drawn to Him. It might be dreams that you have forgotten. Go ahead and write them down, and then commit to praying for them.

_____

_____

_____

_____

Do you have any answer to prayer that you want to record? (You can write it here or in your prayer journal.)

_____

_____

_____

_____

Note

1. George Müller, quoted in Roger Steer, *Delighted in God: A Biography of George Müller* (London, UK: Hodder & Stoughton, 1975), p. 222.

6

Get Alone with God

When you pray, go into your room, close the door and
pray to your Father, who is unseen. Then your Father,
who sees what is done in secret, will reward you.
MATTHEW 6:6

J. O. Frasier left England many years ago to bring the message of Christ's love to the Lisus, an unreached people who lived in the high mountain ranges of western China. The entry to the mountain ranges was at their midpoint, which was the site of a small village outpost. Frasier realized that he would probably be the only missionary to this tribe for years to come. He prayed, "Lord, which way should I go, to the north or to the south?"

Frasier sensed that God wanted him to reach both people groups, so he decided to pray for the southern people—whom he had never met—from sunup to noon and evangelize among the northern people from noon to sundown; this became a pattern he followed for years. The work grew slowly. A few hundred people came to Christ among the people in the north over the course of a decade.

After many years, Frasier left the mountains for a period of rest and to get supplies at the village outpost. Now very familiar with the Lisu language, he heard a Lisu speaking with a different dialect in the marketplace. The man turned out to be a southern Lisu. Frasier struck up a conversation with the man, shared a meal with him and invited him to his rented quarters. He lovingly shared the good news of Christ with him, and the man was quick to respond and accept Jesus as his Lord and Savior.

For several weeks, Frasier tutored the illiterate man, helping him memorize verses from the Bible. He told him story after story from the Bible, praying that the Holy Spirit would help him remember what he was hearing. Finally Frasier sent him on his way, urging him to tell the southern Lisus about Jesus. Frasier returned to the north, the site of his own ministry, praying as usual half of each day for the people in the south.

Many more years passed. Then one day a delegation of southern Lisus arrived at the village Frasier lived in. They reported the news that thousands of southern Lisus had become followers of Christ and were in desperate need for someone to come and teach them more. As tears of joy welled up in his eyes, Frasier realized that his time invested alone in prayer from sunup to noon had reaped a harvest many times greater than his work from noon to sundown.

Jesus said that when we pray, we ought to get alone with God, like J. O. Frasier did for so many hours each day. Jesus said that to be authentic in our prayers, we have to pass two tests: (1) the audience test, and (2) the secrecy test. For *the audience test*, we need to ask ourselves, *Who am I doing this for?* During Jesus' time, the hypocrites prayed and fasted in sight of others, so people would think they were high and holy. Jesus said of them, "And when you pray, do not be like the hypocrites, for they love to pray standing in the synagogues and on the street corners to be seen by men. I tell you the truth, they have received their reward in full" (Matt. 6:5).

Jesus meant that if you pray only so that others will think well of you—for anyone other than God to hear—then being seen by others is all the reward you're going to get. You won't experi-

ence God's incredible peace and supernatural power.

For *the secrecy test*, we need to ask ourselves, *Would I do this if no one saw me?* Jesus said, "When you pray, go into your room, close the door and pray to your Father, who is unseen. Then your Father, who sees what is done in secret, will reward you" (Matt. 6:6). Jesus meant that when you pray, you should not be like the hypocrites. The English word "hypocrite" is a direct transliteration of the Greek word *hupokritai*. During ancient times, this theatrical term described an actor who wore a mask in order to play a part, so he could pretend to be one thing entirely different from that which he was behind the mask. Everybody who heard what Jesus said understood what He was talking about when He used that term; a hypocrite appeared to be something on the outside different from what he was on the inside.

All of us go through a constant battle about what others think of us. We display outwardly what we want others to see and believe about us. We live our lives constantly trying to manage our image. We say and do things so that we can get others to think of us as we want them to think of us. But Jesus said that if you want to be authentic, you have to be the same on the inside as you are on the outside.

I once saw a cartoon about this conflict between public and private appearance. The cartoon showed a wife saying to her pastor husband, "I've got a good idea. How about this week, you be grumpy at church and charming at home?" Evidently there was just a little inconsistency in their lives. I understand this. I can go to church and be kind and warm and winsome, and then come home and be tired and grumpy and impatient.

To make sure we are not two-sided, especially when we pray, Jesus said we should pray in secret. Never pray to impress people. Pray to an audience of one: God.

I'm afraid that for many of us in the Church, this is a practice that has been largely ignored. We live most of our lives in a public setting and seem to always be around other people. This can be disastrous when it comes to prayer. There are, of course, times when the Bible instructs us to pray with others (we will talk about that later in the book). But most of our prayers, Jesus said, should be done in secret. If we pray in secret, Jesus promised that God will reward us openly. In other words, when we get in a room and shut the door to pray, we increase the likelihood of God answering our prayers.

Frasier prayed alone for half a day nearly every day. The results were miraculous. The same thing can happen for you.

THE DARE

Do you see how important your time alone with God in prayer can be? Today's dare is for you to commit yourself right now to spending time alone with God in prayer each day.

Write down the time of day that you plan to get alone with God to pray.

_____

_____

_____

_____

Write down the place that you plan to get alone with God to pray.

_____

_____

_____

_____

How do you think the way you pray will change when you pray alone?

_____

_____

_____

_____

_____

Write down the requests that you would like to ask of God in your time alone with Him. Then write down any answers to prayer that you have already seen. (You can use the space below or your journal. Typically, I record two or three answers to prayer in my journal every day.)

_____

_____

_____

_____

_____

7

Admit that It's Not About You

Our Father in heaven, hallowed by your name, your kingdom come,
your will be done on earth as it is in heaven.
MATTHEW 6:9-10

Some time back, I was at a tennis tournament with our 12-year-old daughter, Cam. Cam made it through the first four rounds of the tournament relatively easily. She had to play a tougher opponent in the final, but she had never lost to this opponent in the past, so she did not anticipate a problem in this match. I arrived late for the match and was a little surprised to find Cam down love-1. *Oh well*, I thought.

Cam won her serve but then lost the other girl's serve again. She was down 1-2. Cam won her next serve in quick order but then lost the other girl's service game once again. She was down 2-3. *At least she will win her serve*, I consoled myself. But then Cam made a couple errors and got down love-30.

Whenever you dig a hole like that, you flirt with danger. Cam threw in a service winner but then made another error. She was down 15-40. She was playing with fire. One more mistake and she would lose the game. Cam won the next point easily. It was 30-40. The next point was a 20-stroke rally. Cam was playing it safely. But then she dropped a shot into the net. All of a sudden, she was down 2-4. This was not going the way we had expected prior to the match. The girls traded punches over the next four games, but Cam ended up losing the set 4-6. This was not the way to start a match Cam had planned on winning easily.

The second set was a totally different story, with Cam shifting into a whole different gear. She started serving harder and hitting more aggressively, and she basically dominated the play. She won the set easily.

Because of time constraints, the third set was a super tiebreaker: The first player to win 10 points would win the set. Normally, players try to avoid having to play such anything-can-happen games, but if a super tiebreaker has to be played, each competitor wants to jump out to a quick lead and dominate play. Cam chose not to do it that way. As the match got tighter and tighter, I found myself praying more and more, "Lord, please help her." As things got still tighter, I got even more desperate, "Pleeease, Lord." (If you put in more vowels, God is more likely to answer.) I said, "Lord, this would be a disaster if she lost this match."

All of a sudden, what I was doing struck me: My prayer was all about me and Cam. I mean, really? A disaster? A disaster for whom? For me? For Cam? For what? Since when is a loss a disaster? Since God is interested in our hearts, our character and our responses to events in our lives, a loss can be just as valuable as a win. I wasn't praying for God's kingdom concerns. I was praying for my own and Cam's concerns. It was all about my pride and ego and Cam's game.

When Jesus taught His disciples the Lord's Prayer, He told them to start by saying, "Our Father in heaven, hallowed be your name, your kingdom come, your will be done on earth as it is in heaven" (Matt. 6:9-10). He said the first concerns of our prayers ought to be *His* name, *His* kingdom and *His* will. I was praying about *my* name, *my* kingdom and *my* will, or Cam's name, Cam's kingdom and Cam's will. (In case you're interested, Cam won the tiebreaker, match and tournament; but it wasn't due to the nobility of my prayers.)

Have you ever found yourself praying the way I did? You pray for a job, to get a promotion, to win an athletic game, to do well on a test or for the weather to be nice for an outing; and suddenly you realize that it's all about you. That's directly opposite what our first concern should be: God and His kingdom concerns. If our prayers are all about us, we turn God into a kind of cosmic errand boy. The first three requests in the Lord's Prayer are not about us but for God's honor to be increased, God's kingdom to be expanded and God's will to be done. To pray this way is to express the priorities of a Christ follower. In our culture, we are constantly taught to be concerned with ourselves, our glory, our kingdom and our will. But a Christ follower's top concerns, Jesus said, are God's name, kingdom and will.

What increases God's kingdom and brings honor to His name? God's will is that His lost children be found, that people everywhere come to worship Him and that His kingdom will reign in the hearts of men and women all over the world. Praying the Lord's Prayer signals your willingness to take part in spreading His kingdom to the people in your sphere of influence. God's will is that your life will shine so brightly with love and purity, that your husband, wife, sister, brother, father, mother, friend, work associate or classmate will be irresistibly drawn to Christ. Do you want to have more power in your prayers? Pray for things that will increase God's honor, kingdom and will.

Although Jesus went on to instruct us to pray for "our daily bread"—to pray for our needs—the context of our prayer is still to be God's kingdom, honor and will. This means that when we pray, we promise to give God the credit when He meets our needs. Why should God answer our prayers if we're going to take the credit ourselves when He answers?

To give God the credit was why I began keeping a prayer journal during college. Every time I made a specific request and God answered it, I recorded it. And I always give Him the credit for the answers, not myself.

THE DARE

For today's dare, I want you to start your prayer time by praying the Lord's Prayer slowly, actually listening to each word and/or phrase, and thinking about what you're praying for. Now think about and answer the following questions.

What were some of the things you felt you should pray about today that would increase God's kingdom and honor and fulfill God's will?

_____

_____

_____

_____

_____

What answers to prayer can you think of from yesterday's prayers?

_____

_____

_____

_____

_____

8

Only by Prayer

[Jesus] replied, "This kind can come out only by prayer."
MARK 9:29

Mark told about a man who came to Jesus and said, "Teacher, I brought you my son, who is possessed by a spirit that has robbed him of speech. Whenever it seizes him, it throws him to the ground. He foams at the mouth, gnashes his teeth and becomes rigid. I asked your disciples to drive out the spirit, but they could not" (Mark 9:17-18).

I think it's clear that the father was frustrated. I am certain he had tried every doctor and priest—anyone and everyone he could find—to help cure his demon-possessed son, but no one had been able to help. When he finally thought he had found someone who could help—Jesus—he brought his son to the town where he expected to find Jesus, only to find that Jesus had gone away. But some of the disciples were there, so he asked them to help his demon-possessed son, but they could not.

When Jesus returned, the man hurried to Him with his request. Jesus proceeded to cast the demon out and heal the boy. Afterward, the disciples asked Jesus why they had been unable to cast the demon from the boy. Jesus responded, "This kind can come out only by prayer" (Mark 9:29). What Jesus meant was that there are matters we encounter in this world that are too big for us, and that those things in life can be dealt with *only by prayer.*

Jim Cymbala, pastor of the Brooklyn Tabernacle in New York, tells about an only-by-prayer situation in his life. When his oldest daughter, Chrissy, was about 18 or 19, she went through a period of serious rebellion. At one point she ran away from home, and Cymbala and his wife did not see her for four months. Naturally, they were worried sick about her. All they knew was that she was living on the streets somewhere. He mentioned his concern for her one week at their church's Tuesday-night prayer meeting. In response to a prompting from the Holy Spirit, a woman passed a note to Jim that said, "I think we should pray for Chrissy." So he had the people pray for her. Hundreds of people cried out to God for her and interceded on her behalf. When they were done, Jim just knew somehow that something had happened.

When he got home, he said to his wife, "If there's a God in heaven, Chrissy is coming home." And that's exactly what happened. The next morning Chrissy came home. In response to the prayers of the previous evening, God nudged Chrissy to come home. When Jim told the congregation the following week that she had come home in answer to their prayers, the people erupted in spontaneous applause. Today Chrissy is married to a pastor, has three children and is serving the Lord. But she came back *only by prayer.*

You may be facing something so overwhelming in your life that you've been stopped in your tracks and you've said, "I don't know what to do." Maybe it's a health crisis. Maybe it's a problem in your marriage, and you're wondering if your marriage is even going to make it. Maybe you're concerned about a son or daughter who has gone astray. Maybe you have a problem with somebody at school or a problem with a parent. Maybe you're facing a struggle at work with a boss, an employee or a co-worker. Maybe you don't have enough income to pay your bills, or maybe you don't have a job at all. Possibly you're struggling with an addiction. Whatever your crisis is, you're so worried about it that you've come to the end of your rope—you're facing an *only-by-prayer* situation.

For several nights in June 1982, the night sky over Beirut looked like the Fourth of July. Francis Scott Key's description of "the rockets' red glare, the bombs bursting in air" seemed to fit the chaos that was taking place. But even those words could not begin to describe the fury unleashed by Israel's bombing of that ravaged port city. Yet in the midst of that rain of bombs, a miracle was taking place. That miracle had its roots in a discussion two University of Oregon students had had three years earlier about how they could tell the school's student body about Christ.

There were only 65 believers on the University of Oregon campus at the time, and these two students wanted to come up with an evangelistic approach that would be innovative, scripturally sound and effective—they wanted to reach the entire student body. Finally they designed a strategy. On a map, they portioned off the university into seven sections. During the next several days they walked around each section, asking God to do what He had promised Joshua: "I will give you every place where you set your foot" (Josh. 1:3). After two months of trudging around campus, stopping to pray in each dormitory and academic department, one student said to the other, "This is ludicrous. If God does not answer prayer, this has sure been a waste of time." But the students continued their treks. Two months later, their prayers were answered when Christian author Josh McDowell spoke on campus. A few years later, the University of Oregon became the most fruitful ministry for Campus Crusade for Christ on the West Coast. God had worked mightily on that campus.

One of the two students who had done the prayer walking became a missionary in Beirut and decided to keep up his prayer walks. He outlined four sections on a map of Muslim West Beirut where he would walk and pray for the homes, the people and the businesses. He had to stop his walks in June 1982 because the war got too dangerous. But when it was safe for him to venture out again, something along his prayer route seemed odd, but at first he couldn't figure out exactly what it was. Then it hit him. The buildings within the routes outlined for his walks remained standing. Buildings just outside those routes had been demolished. If this is what God does in the physical realm when we pray, what does He do in the spiritual realm?

In the kingdom of God, nothing is more important than prayer. Noah prayed, and God handed him a blueprint for the ark of deliverance. Moses prayed, and God delivered the Israelites from Egyptian bondage. Gideon prayed, and a formidable enemy fled before his band of only 300 soldiers. David prayed, and he defeated Goliath. Elijah prayed, and the fire of God consumed the sacrifice and licked up the water around the altar. Daniel prayed, and the mouths of the lions were closed. Jesus said the power of Satan can only be overcome by prayer. People today desperately need the help we can give them. Marriages are being shattered. Children are being destroyed. Individuals are living lives of quiet desperation, without purpose or future. And we can make a difference . . . if we pray on their behalf.

THE DARE

Are you convinced that prayer is vitally important? Jesus said some battles can be won *only by prayer*. How much do you pray for your friends, mate, children, parents, pastor, church, president and leaders? Your prayer dare for today is to take more time for prayer over situations in which you need a miracle that can only come by prayer.

What problems are you encountering that can only be overcome by a miracle through prayer?

_____

_____

_____

_____

_____

What have you learned about prayer the past few days that has been most helpful to you?

_____

_____

_____

_____

_____

9

Recognize the Power in Prayer

*For I know that through your prayers and the help
given by the Spirit of Jesus Christ, what has happened to me
will turn out for my deliverance.*

PHILIPPIANS 1:19

The apostle Paul surprises us. We're not surprised that he said the Spirit of Christ helps us. We know about the importance of the Holy Spirit. What surprises us is that he said, "For I know that through your prayers and the help given by the Spirit of Jesus Christ, what has happened to me will turn out for my deliverance" (Phil. 1:19). Paul said that the people's prayers for him were as necessary to his deliverance as the supply of the Spirit. And he mentions the prayers first. Do you realize that your prayers are that important?

Let me share with you an example of just how important every single prayer can be. This is from a woman in my church, who sent me this story as an example of an answer to prayer from her journal.

Two years ago I climbed up on a concrete ledge in the garage to prune some plants. All of a sudden my foot slipped and I began to fall backwards. All I had time to do was put my hands over the back of my head and pray, "Lord, be with me." All of a sudden I felt as if I was floating, and I landed on the concrete driveway as if it were a soft pillow. I thank the Lord for sparing me from broken bones and from what could have been a fatal fall.

Isn't that amazing? Apparently, God sent an angel to catch her. Amazing things like this happen when we pray. Yet in spite of all the ways God answers prayers, I still don't think most people get how important prayer is.

East Indian evangelist K. P. Yohannan says he will never forget one of his first prayer meetings in an American church. He had come to the United States eager to meet some of its spiritual giants. One man in particular held his interest, a preacher known even in India for his powerful sermons and uncompromising commitment to the truth. More than 3,000 people attended services on the Sunday Yohannan visited this church. The choirs were outstanding and the preaching was everything he'd hoped it would be. But he was especially taken by an announcement the pastor made about the special emphasis he wanted to ask for at the upcoming midweek prayer meeting. He said there were some things lying heavy on his heart, and he asked if the people would come and pray about them. Then he announced the name of a certain chapel on the church campus. Excited, Yohannan determined he would attend.

When he arrived at the chapel later that week, he brought with him some definite assumptions about prayer meetings. The most basic of his assumptions was that prayer meetings are essential and actually of primary importance. Where he came from in India—and in many other parts of the world where Christians are persecuted and harassed for their faith—the prayer meeting is the centerpiece of the church's life. Everyone comes, the meetings often last long into the night, and it is not unusual for believers to arise daily before sunup to pray together for the work of the church.

Fearing a huge crowd, he came early to get a seat. But when he arrived, he was surprised to discover a chapel with a capacity for only 500—and it was empty! He thought that surely he had heard the pastor wrong and had come to the wrong place. He was worried enough that he went outside to double-check the name of the chapel. Then some people came into the room at 7:30, but there was no leader, no songs and no worship; he just heard chitchat about news, weather and sports. Forty-five minutes later, an elderly man, evidently the prayer-meeting leader, walked into the chapel to offer a few devotional thoughts from the Bible and give a brief prayer. The meeting was over; and as the seven attendees filed out of the chapel, K. P. Yohannan sat in stunned silence, his mind filled with questions: *Was this it? Where were the tears? What about that burden that the pastor said was heavy on his heart? Weren't we going to intercede for a miracle? And where was the pastor?*[1]

Yohannan had been shocked by the low priority prayer was in that church, yet what he experienced is pretty typical for American churches. In the 30 years I have been the pastor of Sunset Presbyterian Church, almost every time I have made a call for prayer, I have been disappointed with the turnout.

I firmly believe that the reason for such low prayer-meeting turnouts is that we fail to recognize the power in prayer. When we desire something for ourselves or for others, something that is beyond our power to give, we must remember to pray to God. God *does* have the power—even to move mountains.

THE DARE

Have you ever been in a disastrous situation? What did you do? Was your first thought to pray to God? Your dare today is to ask God to move a mountain. It could be for a family member, a friend, or yourself. Keep praying.

What "mountain" do you need God to move?

_____

_____

_____

_____

_____

Have you been relying on your own strength to move it? If so, in what ways?

_____

_____

_____

_____

How will things change now that you know that God has the power and is the one who can move that mountain?

_____

_____

_____

_____

_____

Note

1. Ben Patterson, *Deepening Your Conversation with God* (Minneapolis, MN: Bethany House, 1999), pp. 158-159.

10

Prayer Is About What Jesus Did

Therefore, since we have a great high priest who has gone through the heavens, Jesus the Son of God, let us hold firmly to the faith we profess.
HEBREWS 4:14

A few weeks ago I didn't have a great week with my wife. For starters, it was very busy. On the weekend, I took our eighth-grade daughter to an out-of-town tennis tournament. Jorie stayed home and took our sixth-grade daughter to a gymnastics meet in Portland. During the week I had several evening meetings, so I was gone a lot. When I was home, I was so preoccupied with things I had to get done that I did not spend much time with my wife. I did not do a great job communicating with Jorie about stuff I had going on, so we had one or two miscues in the schedule. Then I did something that was hurtful to Jorie. It all caught up to me toward the end of the week when I needed something from Jorie. My request had no sooner left my lips that I realized the timing was bad. I had been gone and hadn't been meeting her needs, and I realized I wasn't in a very good position to ask her for anything.

Have you ever had that happen to you? You need something from a parent or spouse, but you haven't done what that person has asked of you. You need something from your employer, but you haven't finished an assignment. You need something from a friend, but you haven't been much of a friend lately.

The same thing can happen in our relationship with God. You need something from God, but you realize you haven't been spending much time with Him and haven't done some of the things He's asked you to do, so you don't feel confident in making requests of Him.

However, the author of Hebrews reminded us: "Therefore, since we have a great high priest who has gone through the heavens, Jesus the Son of God, let us hold firmly to the faith we profess" (Heb. 4:14). What did the writer of Hebrews know about God and prayer that we don't?

First off, let's remember whom this is about. Prayer is about God. Jesus is fully God and He is the Son of God. God sent His Son to die for all our sins. Because Jesus died for all our sins, God washed our slate clean, and you and I don't stand guilty before God. We don't stand in need of punishment before we can speak to God. Jesus took our punishment for us. We can approach God through prayer, because Jesus died for our sins, rose from the dead and went *through the heavens* into the very presence of God, where He sits at the right hand of God, interceding for us.

Isaiah said, "Your iniquities have separated you from your God; your sins have hidden his face from you, so that he will not hear" (Isa. 59:2). You might think that our sins keep us apart from God, so that He cannot hear us. Does God refuse to listen to us when we're living in sin? That can't be true. If it were true, how would God hear the cry of an unbeliever? What Isaiah meant was that when we are harboring sin, we feel so crummy about ourselves and so embarrassed, we do not bring our requests to God. But now that Jesus has paid the penalty for our sins, our record has been wiped clean.

The fact that Jesus paid for our sins and that we have a clean slate doesn't mean that we can live any way we want. When we're

not obeying God, we instinctively feel as if we don't have the right to ask God for anything, just like I felt that day with my wife. Our sins don't keep God from hearing us, but they keep us from asking, because we feel embarrassed. All we have to do is confess our sins. We have to come clean with God every day when we pray.

But what did the writer of Hebrews mean by "hold firmly to the faith we profess"? We are to seize the faith that if we want to pray for something, we shouldn't start by reciting all the good things we have done and why God owes us. That will never work. We need to start by reminding ourselves what Jesus did. When you give your life to Christ and come to God in prayer, Jesus, our representative, says to the Father, "This one is Mine. His penalty is paid. He has accepted My death on his behalf."

THE DARE

When you pray, don't come with the attitude that because you've been good, God owes you something. Don't start by reciting all the good things you've done, as if that could impress God and bully Him into giving you what you want. Admit that you don't deserve anything. Base your confidence on what Jesus did for you on the cross. Because God poured all His punishment against sin out on Jesus, He can extend mercy to you.

Today, ask God for something simply because He is merciful—even if you think you don't deserve it. Record your prayer . . . if you dare.

_____

_____

_____

_____

_____

Why should you feel more confident praying on the basis of God's mercy rather than on the basis of your own goodness?

_____

_____

_____

_____

_____

As we go on, when you experience any answers to prayer, remember to go back and record them.

11

Pray with Confidence

For we do not have a high priest who is unable to sympathize with our weaknesses, but we have one who has been tempted in every way, just as we are—yet was without sin. Let us then approach the throne of grace with confidence, so that we may receive mercy and find grace to help us in our time of need.
HEBREWS 4:15-16

A Christian rancher in Montana had a son who had a heart attack and was whisked into the hospital for emergency open-heart surgery. While the surgeon worked on his son, the rancher sat in the waiting room, praying. He earnestly pleaded with God to spare his son. After about two hours of surgery, the surgeon trudged out to the waiting room with slumped shoulders and spoke quietly to the father. "I'm sorry. We did everything we could for your son, but he didn't make it."

The father replied, "No, doctor, you're wrong. While I was out here praying, God assured me that my son was going to come through the surgery just fine. So you get back in there and do whatever you have to do to save him." At the insistence of the rancher, the surgeon went back into the operating room.

A couple hours later, the doctor emerged with a big smile on his face. He grinned to the father, "You know something? You were right. We were able to resuscitate your son, and his heart is doing fine."

Don't you wonder how the father had such confidence to speak to the surgeon as he did?

I think we might find an answer in the book of Hebrews. As we learned in the last chapter, because God poured out all His punishment against sin on His Son, Jesus, the penalty for our sins has been paid; now, Jesus intercedes for us, so we can approach God in prayer (see Heb. 4:14). The author of Hebrews then described Jesus and how we should approach God:

> For we do not have a high priest who is unable to sympathize with our weaknesses, but we have one who has been tempted in every way, just as we are—yet was without sin. Let us then approach the throne of grace with confidence, so that we may receive mercy and find grace to help us in our time of need (Heb. 4:15-16).

Notice the "then." "Then" refers to what the author has already said, the reason for our confidence in prayer: Jesus, our high priest. After telling us that Jesus is a great high priest who has gone through the heavens and is the Son of God in verse 14, why did the writer change from the positive to the negative in the beginning of verse 15? I think it is because the writer was aware that someone might think that because Jesus is the Son of God, He is too remote from us—He is so high in heaven that He cannot understand our needs. But the writer hastened to dispel this concern by saying that Jesus was perfectly qualified for His role as our high priest because He was not only fully God, but He was also fully man.

There were two qualifications for a priest during the time of the Old Testament. The first was that he be called by God. Jesus fulfilled this qualification by being appointed by God to take the punishment for our sins; and, more than that, He was God Himself.

The second qualification for a priest was kinship. The priest had to identify with the people. "Every high priest is selected from among men and is appointed to represent them in matters related to God. . . . He is able to deal gently with those who are ignorant and are going astray, since he himself is subject to weakness" (Heb. 5:1-2). Jesus fulfilled this qualification because, having been a man, He could sympathize with us.

The original Greek word translated as "sympathize" in Hebrews 4:15 means to "suffer along with." Christ suffered along with us. He was tempted in every way that we are. He understands us. He went through it, so He knows what you and I are going through.

You have to know your history to recognize how staggering the writer's claim is that Jesus was fully human. The Jews emphasized the holiness of God, how different God was from us. The Greek Stoics spoke of gods who had no feelings. They were above feelings. The Epicureans conceived of gods that were completely detached from the world. For centuries, people thought of God as untouchable. Then along came Jesus Christ, and we find a God who loves us so much that He became a man and fully entered into our world, experiencing all the temptations we face and all the suffering we endure.

Now some people complain that since Jesus was God, His temptations must not have really been a test. But that is simply not true. Christ endured depths of temptation that you and I will never know. We fall to temptation long before the tempter has put all of his weapons in play. When Christ was tempted, the tempter put his entire arsenal into action. Yet Christ was victorious. That's why the author of Hebrews added that Jesus "yet was without sin." Sympathy with us as sinners in our trials does not depend on the experience of sin but on the experience of the strength of the temptation to sin that only the sinless can know in its full intensity. It is because Jesus endured all the temptation that you and I face (and more) that He is able to forgive us and be merciful to us. The best person to give you advice and help on a journey is someone who has traveled the road before you. Jesus can help because He was there and knows it all.

So why can we pray with confidence? Because we come to a "throne of grace." We're not coming to a God who says, "What have you done to earn my favor? What have you done for me this week?" We come to a God who, because He poured out all His judgment against sin on His Son, can be gracious and merciful to us. He gives us grace in our time of need.

The rancher knew this. He knew that he prayed to a God who knew the pain of losing a son. He knew that he prayed to a God who is both powerful and merciful. So he prayed with confidence.

THE DARE

When you pray today, start by recognizing that Jesus knows everything you're going through and more. He sympathizes with you. He's been through it. There is nothing you're bringing to Him that He doesn't already understand. Because of this, you don't have to be afraid to tell Him anything, and you don't have to be afraid to ask Him for anything. He has all the power in the world and all the mercy in the world.

Today, I want you to pray with confidence, because you are coming to a throne of grace and mercy. You are coming to Jesus, who understands what you are going through. Try praying

this way today: "Dear Jesus, I'm asking you to be gracious to me, because you have been through what I am facing. You have the power to change this situation."

Record what you prayed here or in your prayer journal.

_____

_____

_____

_____

_____

How did it feel to ask Jesus to be merciful?

_____

_____

_____

_____

Praise God First

> *"O LORD, God of our fathers, are you not the God who is in heaven?*
> *You rule over all the kingdoms of the nations. Power and might are in*
> *your hand, and no one can withstand you."*
> 2 CHRONICLES 20:6

Today we come to a subject I cannot possibly overemphasize when it comes to prayer: praise. Whatever your prayers look like, make sure there is praise in them. Lots of it. And one of the experts on this subject was Jehoshaphat.

Jehoshaphat ruled as the king of Judah from about 873 to 847 BC. Jehoshaphat's reign was not an easy one, for "the Moabites and Ammonites with some of the Meunites came to make war on [him]" (2 Chron. 20:1). The Ammonites and Moabites occupied what we know today as Jordan and the West Bank. The Meunites lived due south of Israel and east of the Dead Sea. Jehoshaphat faced the combined armies of enemies from all around Judah. He was in a desperate situation. So what did he do? He prayed. What I want you to notice is how he started his prayer: "O LORD, God of our fathers, are you not the God who is in heaven? You rule over all the kingdoms of the nations. Power and might are in your hand, and no one can withstand you" (2 Chron. 20:6). Even though he was in a nearly impossible situation, he praised God, telling God that His authority extended over all kingdoms and over all heaven and earth.

Almost all of the greatest prayers in the Bible begin in praise. Why is praise so important? When we begin our prayers in praise, we renew our confidence that God is able to deal with whatever situation we face. That is why Jesus instructed us to begin the Lord's Prayer with "Our Father in heaven." We remind ourselves that we are praying to the God who loves us like a father and rules over heaven and earth.

Most of us offer far too little praise in our prayers. We jump right into our requests. But Scripture commands us to praise God. The apostle Paul said, "Rejoice in the Lord always: and again I say, Rejoice" (Phil. 4:4, *KJV*). He wrote, "Rejoice evermore" (1 Thess. 5:16, *KJV*). The writer of Hebrews instructed, "Through Jesus, therefore, let us continually offer to God a sacrifice of praise—the fruit of lips that confess his name" (Heb. 13:15). Praise should constantly be on our lips. God loves to receive our praise. Like the proud mother who is thrilled to receive a wilted bouquet of dandelions from her child, God celebrates our most feeble attempts at praise.

When my wife and I pray together, it's not uncommon for the first 15 minutes of our prayer to be nothing but praise. And one time in particular, praise really helped us.

Seven months after bringing home our youngest daughter from Vietnam, Erikaa was diagnosed with severe athetoid cerebral palsy. Best guess was that something happened to her at birth. We were crushed by the news. We were devastated that Erikaa would never be able to run and play sports. Because she wouldn't be able to talk, kids would probably think she was stupid and make fun of her. Why did God allow this to happen? He is all-powerful. Surely He could have done something to prevent this disability.

After a week or two of being stunned by the news, we decided that God was still God and that He knew what He was doing. So we decided to again praise God. In fact, we determined to praise God for giving us Erikaa. We made up our minds that we would not focus on her limitations and be distraught about her condition but that we would praise God for giving us a wonderful daughter. We chose to praise God for all the things she could do, rather than lamenting what she couldn't do. And we discovered that praising God brought about in us a whole new attitude.

We began to notice what a delight Erikaa is. She has actually changed our whole family for the better. Our whole family has developed a whole new sensitivity toward people with disabilities. She has engendered a new tenderness in all of us and has caused our whole family to become more joyful and loving. Everyone looks forward to hugging her and hearing her laugh when they come home. At this point, if we could turn back the clock nine years and change her diagnosis, I'm not sure any of us would want to do so. She has been such a wonderful gift to us just the way she is. God's promise is true: "All things work together for good" (Rom. 8:28, *KJV*).

We just need to remember to praise God for whatever our situation is. Praise is powerful stuff.

THE DARE

In spite of whatever troubles you have, from now on start every prayer with praise for who God is. Like Jehoshaphat did, praise God for His power and authority. Praise God for all the blessings He has bestowed on you. (Maybe by the time you're done, you won't feel a need to bring any requests to God. You will be so convinced that God is more than a match for any troubles you face, you will hardly feel a need to mention them.) Now answer the questions below.

What are some of the reasons God deserves your praise? What has He already done for you?

_____

_____

_____

_____

_____

Describe a difficult situation you're in, a personal issue you have to deal with. What blessings can you find in what you're facing?

_____

_____

_____

_____

_____

13

Praise Instills Confidence in Us

Jehoshaphat bowed with his face to the ground, and all the people
of Judah and Jerusalem fell down in worship before the LORD.
Then some Levites from the Kohathites and Korahites stood up and
praised the LORD, the God of Israel, with a very loud voice.
2 CHRONICLES 20:18-19

Jehoshaphat and the people of Judah were surrounded by an
army somewhere between three to six times the size of their
army. With such a formidable force before him, the king could
easily have been terrified, maybe even depressed. He was un-
doubtedly filled with all kinds of troubling emotions. But Jehoshaphat stood before the people and offered a prayer to God
that began with praise. He reminded himself and the people
that God is far greater than the armies that stood against them.
He admitted to God that they had no power to take on their
enemies, so he asked God to intervene. God was pleased with
Jehoshaphat's praise and his humble admission that he could
do nothing without God, so He sent word through the prophet
Jahaziel that He would answer Jehoshaphat's prayer. All who
heard this pronouncement reacted immediately:

> Jehoshaphat bowed with his face to the ground, and all
> the people of Judah and Jerusalem fell down in worship
> before the Lord. Then some Levites from the Kohathites

and Korahites stood up and praised the Lord, the God of Israel, with a very loud voice (2 Chron. 20:18-19).

Understand that the enemy armies were not yet defeated. Nevertheless, Jehoshaphat and the people offered God worship and praise. They believed God and chose to praise Him for what He would do.

That's what God wants from us. He wants us to trust Him and praise Him, even though we may face very difficult circumstances. When we praise God, our attitude is changed. That's what happened to Jehoshaphat, as his leadership was transformed the very next day:

> Early in the morning they left for the Desert of Tekoa. As they set out, Jehoshaphat stood and said, "Listen to me, Judah and the people of Jerusalem! Have faith in the LORD your God and you will be upheld; have faith in his prophets and you will be successful (2 Chron. 20:20).

God's answer to Jehoshaphat's praise transformed Jehoshaphat into a strong and confident leader.

One Sunday I was preaching on this very subject, the power of praise. The Thursday before I had been thinking about all the challenges facing me. Rather than complaining to God about the difficulties I faced at home and the problems I encountered at work, I decided I would put my sermon into practice and focus my prayers on praising God for who He is and thanking Him for all the good things He had already done in my family and in our church. Since I was alone, I felt free to sing to God. Thanksgivings poured forth from my lips for many things, great and small. As I prayed, I found my attitude changing from worry and fear to hope and courage. As I reminded myself of what God had already done, I gained a new sense of confidence about the future.

Do you see why praise is so important to our prayers? Praise changes us, because it focuses our minds on the greatness and goodness of God: "It is good to praise the LORD and make music to your name, O Most High, to proclaim your love in the morning and your faithfulness at night" (Ps. 92:1). Praise is good for us, for it reminds us that God is strong enough to do whatever we need and loves us enough to do whatever is best for us. Knowing and acknowledging that builds our confidence.

One day I was really frustrated with our fifth son, Mark. He was six at the time and was a hyperactive child, always busy doing things, not all of them good. This particular Saturday he had locked himself in the bathroom, apparently to try out a razor he had found lying around. When he emerged, he had several bald spots on his head. He looked ridiculous. But I had to do some grocery shopping, so I took him with me. As I was paying for our groceries, the clerk looked at Mark and then said to me, "Playing with the scissors, I see."

"Razor," I corrected her.

"You know why God made him so cute, don't you?" she asked. "To keep him alive!"

As I headed to the car, I noticed how cute Mark was and what a happy kid he was. I decided that instead of thinking about how much he challenged and frustrated me and how earlier that day I had felt like strangling him, I would praise God for him. I praised God for giving us Mark. I praised God for what a fun son He had given us. I praised God that Mark was so smart. I praised God that Mark had given his life to Christ. I praised God that he was healthy and strong. Choosing to praise God for those few minutes transformed my attitude toward Mark. My confidence in Mark grew.

You see, praise not only pleases God, but it also builds us up by instilling confidence in us.

THE DARE

How confident do you feel to face any challenge or frustration that comes your way? How do you usually deal with such situations? Today I want you to think about your greatest challenges and frustrations in a new way. Instead of complaining to God about them, think of all the things you can praise God for in those situations. List your problems, and then praise God.

_____

_____

_____

_____

How has praising God begun to change your attitude toward your difficult situations?

_____

_____

_____

_____

How can praising God make you more confident to face any challenge or frustration in the future?

_____

_____

_____

_____

14

Make Praise a Lifestyle

Praise the LORD. Praise the name of the LORD;
praise him, you servants of the LORD.
PSALM 135:1

I know what you're thinking. *Didn't we just talk about praise in the last two chapters?* Yes, but I told you, we cannot possibly overemphasize praise. If all you've gleaned so far is that you should begin your prayers with praise and remind yourself that God is big enough to handle all your problems, I will not be satisfied. I want praise to become the biggest element in your prayers; in fact, I want praise to become more important than your requests. I'm hoping that praise will bring you a *brand-new attitude* toward life. I want this to be a life-changer.

How do we get to the place where we spend more time praising God during our prayers than making requests of Him? How do we get to the place where we begin every day with praise and keep an attitude of praise with us throughout the day? Let me tell you how I've done it.

I've made a covenant with God that I want to begin each day with praise. I try to make praise of God my first thoughts and first words in the morning. I've determined that I want to wake up happy, not grumpy. There are 11 people in my household, and I have learned that some of them wake up happy and some wake up grumpy. I want to be one of the happy ones.

I've also covenanted that all my prayers will begin with praise. That's just the way I start my prayers.

In order to have an attitude of praise throughout the day (and I'm not saying I've mastered this one), I've learned that I have to slow down and notice the little things. I am a driven person. I tend to get so busy with all my plans for the day that I miss God's overtures of love. The demands of home, family, school and work conspire to make life a blur. When I'm breathlessly running on the treadmill of life, I overlook the little things God does. I cannot adore Him when I do not see Him. If I am moving too quickly, I can be blinded to the beauty that exists all around me: the flower blooming by my doorstep, the wind rustling through the leaves, the moon rising on the horizon, the sun setting behind the hills.

We live in the country. We have bobcats, cougars, deer, squirrels, elk and moles. Lots of moles. I don't praise God for them. I do praise God, however, for a herd of 80 elk who visit our property on average once a week. I always look forward to their coming, and I always stop and look at them when they show up. I consciously try to stop several times each day to notice the little things that are mine to enjoy.

Deitrich Bonhoeffer, in his classic *Life Together*, writes, "Only he who gives thanks for the little things receives the big things. How can God entrust great things to one who will not thankfully receive from him the little things?" If you want to increase power in your prayers, praise God for the many little things He does as well as the big things. Along the way, you'll notice your life begin to change because you've developed a positive attitude.

Some people are negative thinkers. You say to them, "Beautiful day today, isn't it?" They respond, "First nice day we've had all year." Or "It's too hot. It stirs up my allergies." I try to watch

myself, because I don't want to be that way. I believe it dishonors God, who gave us life to enjoy. The psalmist wrote, "Praise the LORD. Praise the name of the LORD; praise him, you servants of the LORD" (Ps. 135:1). Praise helps us be positive thinkers, because it reminds us that God is fully in control. Fixing our minds on God's power gives us a whole new perspective about whatever difficulties we may be facing.

Alan McGinnis, author of *The Friendship Factor*, was on a plane one night before Thanksgiving. He was sitting next to a jolly salesman. This man had been flying all day from upstate New York and had been stranded for the evening in Salt Lake City. Because of the delay, he would not arrive home in Bakersfield until 2 A.M. But was he irritable like most of the travelers in the packed plane? No, he was happy, teasing two little children across the aisle, spreading good cheer to the people.

> "What do you sell?" Alan asked.
>
> "Oil drilling tools."
>
> "That's a tough business to be in these days, isn't it?"
>
> "No," he replied. "It couldn't be better. We just opened another branch office this year and it's doing great."
>
> "But isn't the oil business in a terrible recession?"
>
> "Yes, but we've decided not to participate," he said with a smile. He went on to explain their success. "The industry slump has worked to our advantage because all our competitors are down in the mouth and complaining that they have to cut prices and can't make any money. That negative attitude rubs off on the customers. We, on the other hand, are not cutting our prices at all. But we're giving the best

service of anybody in the industry, we're enthusiastic about our products, and we're very upbeat. Customers like doing business with sales people who have that attitude." He smiled again, and said, "If this recession will just continue one more year, I'll make enough money to retire."[1]

Cultivating a positive attitude obviously helped this man succeed.

I think the reason praise is such a game changer is because it releases the power of God. When Jehoshaphat and his people began to sing and praise God, "The LORD set ambushes against the men of Ammon and Moab and Mount Seir who were invading Judah, and they were defeated" (2 Chron. 20:22). It was when they sang praises that God confused their enemies. Praise sends the powers of darkness scattering and releases the power of God in our lives.

Paul and Silas were once thrown in prison for preaching Christ and delivering a young girl from demon possession (her owners had gotten angry because she could no longer help them become rich through her fortune telling). Most people thrown in prison would be pretty upset. Not Paul and Silas:

> About midnight Paul and Silas were praying and singing hymns to God, and the other prisoners were listening to them. Suddenly there was such a violent earthquake that the foundations of the prison were shaken. At once all the prison doors flew open, and everybody's chains came loose (Acts 16:25–26).

It was when Paul and Silas sang and praised God that God shook the prison and released the prisoners from their chains. Praise will release that same power of God in our lives.

THE DARE

Your challenge today is to make a covenant with God to start each day with praise to Him. Maybe you will need to put a note on your cell phone or clock. You should also ask Him to help you praise Him throughout the day. Commit to slow down and notice the little things God does each day.

What are some of the little things that God gives you today—the blessings that, if you are not careful, you will take for granted and fail to notice? Write these below.

_____

_____

_____

_____

_____

What do you need to do so that you will have time to notice all of the blessings that God is giving to you? (An example would be to take 20 minutes after work). Write this plan below.

_____

_____

_____

_____

_____

Note
1. Alan McGinnis, *The Friendship Factor* (San Francisco: Harper & Row, 1990), p. 85.

15

Corporate Praise

When they heard this, they raised their voices together in
prayer to God. After they prayed, the place where they were
meeting was shaken. And they were all filled with the Holy Spirit
and spoke the word of God boldly.
ACTS 4:24,31

It was a phone call I didn't want to make. I had bad news to tell
Jorie. I had been in Romania for a week, waiting to finalize our
adoption of Andrea, a beautiful girl that Jorie had chosen for us
to adopt from a Bucharest orphanage.

I did not have an opportunity to meet the darling two-
month-old baby girl on our first trip to Romania because while
Jorie visited orphanages, I was busy fulfilling an invitation to
preach in four different cities. Because Romania required both
prospective parents to see the child in country in order to finalize the adoption overseas, there I was, two months later, in
Romania to see our prospective daughter, complete the adoption and bring her home.

I flew the baby's 17-year-old birth mother into Bucharest
for our court appearance, but she asked if she could first go to
the orphanage with me to see baby Andrea. I consented. It was
a mistake. She spent most of the day with Andrea and me as
Andrea's medical tests were completed; and as she held tiny Andrea, I watched her fall in love with the adorable baby she

hadn't cuddled since the day she had given birth to her weeks earlier. By the day's end, I feared that the wonderful time she had had with Andrea might cause her to change her mind and back out of the adoption.

The next morning my worst fears were confirmed. The birth mom had run away, deciding against going through with the adoption. I was really discouraged. I felt as if the long trip and all my efforts that week had been wasted. My heart was very heavy as I picked up the phone to call Jorie with the heart-breaking news.

To my surprise, Jorie did not sound shaken. She assured me that she and our five boys would pray that the birth mom would be found and agree that it was in her best interest and the baby's to go ahead with the adoption. Jorie, and our three oldest boys, Tad, David and Luke, fasted and prayed, as did several friends in our church. Our 12-year-old, Tad, told me later, "I thought I was going to die during that day of fasting." (No food for a day is a big deal for a young kid.)

With all of this prayer support, things began to change in Romania. The depression that had hung over me like a dark cloud lifted. I felt a renewed sense of hope. Three days later, the birth mom was located at her home in northern Romania. She once again agreed that it would be best to go through with the adoption, and a new court date was set. After a total of 17 days in country, I finally flew home with Andrea.

What made the difference? Corporate praise of God. People were praying for Andrea and me, and God moved on our behalf.

Two people praising God together or praying together wield more power than one person alone. It's like Dave Matthews of the Dave Matthews Band sings in one of his songs: "The two of us together can do anything." Two always do better than one.

Scripture has many examples of groups of people praising God in prayer in order to effect a change. One such example of the power believers can experience when they pray together is found in Acts 4. The apostles Peter and John had been thrown in prison by the Jewish establishment, because the Jewish leaders felt threatened by the fact that so many Jews in Jerusalem were beginning to follow Jesus. Because Peter and John had healed a crippled beggar in the name of Jesus, the leaders now feared that there would be even more believers.

The authorities, though, could not hold Peter and John in prison indefinitely, so they let them go with a warning not to preach about Jesus.

After their release, Peter and John told the other believers everything the Jewish religious leaders had said. The reaction of the believers was immediate: "When they heard this, they raised their voices together in prayer to God. After they prayed, the place where they were meeting was shaken. And they were all filled with the Holy Spirit and spoke the word of God boldly" (Acts 4:24,31). God demonstrated His pleasure with their prayer by shaking the building and filling the believers with the Holy Spirit, so they could share the news about Jesus with boldness.

Why did their prayers wield such power? Because they had prayed together. But it wasn't just any kind of prayer. Together they began to praise God: "Sovereign Lord, you made the heaven and the earth and the sea, and everything in them" (Acts 4:24). If you read their entire prayer, you'll find that most of it was praise of God for His greatness (see Acts 4:24-30).

The young church prayed together with praise to God again when King Herod terrorized the fledgling church. First he killed James, the brother of John. Then he booked Peter for an execution. He threw Peter in jail, assigning 16 men to guard him. What did the Early Church do? They prayed. "Peter was kept in prison, but the church was earnestly praying to God for him" (Acts 12:5).

In response to their prayers, God sent an angel to rescue Peter, who was so surprised that he thought he was just seeing a vision. But when the angel left him alone after getting him out of the prison and into the city, he recognized that an angel really had delivered him.

> When this had dawned on him, he went to the house of Mary the mother of John, also called Mark, where many people had gathered and were praying. Peter knocked at the outer entrance, and a servant girl named Rhoda came to answer the door. When she recognized Peter's voice, she was so overjoyed she ran back without opening it and exclaimed, "Peter is at the door!" (Acts 12:12-14).

What did the believers say to Rhoda when they heard her news? " 'You're out of your mind,' they told her" (Acts 12:15).

We tend to think we can never experience power in prayer like the Early Church. We imagine the first Christians as larger than life. We assume they never doubted. But in reading Acts, we learn that they were not much different from us. They prayed but did not really believe God was going to answer their prayers. (Sound familiar?) The Early Church didn't have enough influence to get Peter out of prison, but they had enough power to praise him out. Like these early believers, we don't have to have unwavering faith to pray with power. We just need enough faith to pray. When we praise God with other believers, we have far more power than we realize.

THE DARE

Today, I want you to take an inventory of your life. Are you praising God with other believers? If you're married, are you praising God with your mate? If not, I suggest that you do so. Do you have children? Are you praising God with them? Do you have a friend with whom you can praise God? Ask him or her. Are you in a small group where you can praise God with other Christians? If not, take steps to get in one. You have too many big things at stake in your life for you to be going it alone.

If your answer to any of the questions above was no, what change will you make so that you can join others to praise God?

_____

_____

_____

_____

_____

What are some of the names of people you know with whom you can praise God?

_____

_____

_____

_____

_____

16

Deal with Your Sin

If I had cherished sin in my heart, the Lord would not have listened.
PSALM 66:18

Years ago, *The Chicago Tribune* offered readers a chance to make public confessions of things that were bothering them. The editors of the paper did this because they suspected that people were suffering from things that weighed heavy on their conscience. What they did not anticipate was the volume of people that would respond and the types of things that they would reveal.

One woman confessed that during the four months she was trapped in the same house as her husband during their divorce proceedings, she cleaned all three toilets in the house with a washcloth, which she dutifully hung by her husband's clean towel.

Another woman admitted testing the truthfulness of a friend in a very unusual way. Turns out the woman had come into her friend's kitchen one day with an armload of sweet corn and had screamed in panic when she saw a spider on herself. George, the friend, had ignored her screams, later claiming that he had not seen the spider or he would have brushed it off. She did not believe him and decided to test his eyesight by putting five fishing worms on an open-faced hamburger, which George proceeded to eat, apparently without seeing the worms. She said she had not intended to let him eat the worms, but an unrelated family crisis of sorts distracted her, which made it impossible for her to tell George about the worms and prevent him from eating them.

There are probably a lot of us who have done things surreptitiously that we need to get off our conscience, and it is just such a clearing of our conscience—our confession of our sins—that we need in order to have effective prayers. As the psalmist pointed out, "If I had cherished sin in my heart, the Lord would not have listened" (Ps. 66:18).

In the previous chapters, I told you to begin your prayers with praise. Today I want to explore confession, another element you need to include in your prayers. You want to clear up anything you've thought or done wrong since your last prayer before praying further. As I've already told you, I begin my prayers with praise. Then I confess my sins. And trust me, I have plenty to confess.

A dozen years ago Jorie and I took our family, which included seven kids at the time, and Jorie's mom on a trip to Disneyland. We rented a 15-passenger van to drive down the I-5 corridor from Oregon to Los Angeles; and I had been fortunate to get, through a friend, a special deal on some rooms at the Anaheim Marriott. When we finally reached the hotel, I walked in to get our rooms and found the lobby teaming with high school kids (they were members of marching bands from high schools up and down the West Coast who had come to play in the Rose Parade). Undaunted, I strolled up to the counter and said, "Checking in—Kincaid."

The receptionist got on her computer to look up our reservation. She then excused herself for a moment and went to whisper to a man who was probably her supervisor. He looked on the computer; and then, looking a bit embarrassed, he said to me, "Sir, we don't have a reservation for you."

I said, "What? That's impossible! The reservation was made several months ago!" I didn't have any paperwork with me, because a friend who works for the Marriott chain told me months earlier that he would make a reservation for us.

I felt myself getting angry. To drive a family of 10 for 18 hours only to be told that our reservation had been lost was very upsetting. I said to the manager, "Look, I've always been impressed with the Marriott; what are you going to do to make this right?"

The two conferred for a bit. Then they turned to me, profusely apologized again and then had us escorted to the top floor to the only rooms they still had available: two beautiful penthouse suites, the best rooms in the hotel. They even had a big basket of fruit and candy placed in each room as a peace offering. We had a great time.

A few days after we returned home, I called my friend to tell him what had happened. He said, "Oh no! It wasn't the Anaheim Marriott—I made your reservation at the Fullerton Marriott."

Now it was my turn to be embarrassed—and humiliated. I thought back to the scene I had made at the Anaheim reception desk, where it turns out I never had a reservation. I realized that this was one of the stupidest things I had ever done. I asked my friend to forgive me for all the trouble I had caused him, because he had made the reservation in his name.

Since that vacation worked out so well, I no longer make hotel reservations when we go on trips. I just march into any hotel I want and go berserk if they don't have a reservation for me. (Just kidding!)

Usually when something goes wrong, we don't like to admit our part in it. We like to blame others for what *they* did wrong. But I needed to confess my wrongdoing much the same way Nehemiah confessed his part in his situation: "I confess the sins we Israelites, including myself and my father's house, have committed against you. We have acted very wickedly toward you. We have not obeyed the commands, decrees and laws you gave your servant Moses" (Neh. 1:6-7). Nehemiah not only confessed the sins of Israel, but he also confessed his personal part in those sins.

So we should begin our prayers with praise and then move on to confession. When we leave sins unconfessed, our confidence is destroyed in bringing our requests to God. "Why should God do what I want when I don't do what He wants?" So, first praise, and then confess. It's a simple pattern to follow.

THE DARE

Today, after you have praised God, confess your sins to Him. These could be things you've done, said or just thought. Tell God that you are sorry, admit that you were wrong, and then ask Him to forgive you.

Why is it important to confess your sins before going any further in your prayers?

_____

_____

_____

_____

What are some sins you need to confess? What have you done wrong? What should you have done that you didn't do?

_____

_____

_____

_____

17

Deal with the Sin of Others

*If you forgive men when they sin against you, your heavenly
Father will also forgive you. But if you do not forgive men their sins, your
Father will not forgive your sins.*
MATTHEW 6:14-15

One of the most sobering lines ever to fall from the lips of Jesus
concerned our need to forgive people, if we hope to be forgiven by
God: "If you forgive men when they sin against you, your heavenly
Father will also forgive you. But if you do not forgive men their
sins, your Father will not forgive your sins" (Matt. 6:14-15). Just
reading this throws me into a panic. I think of all the people who
have wronged me that I don't feel very good about. And I'm pretty
sure I'm not going to be exchanging Christmas gifts with these
people this year. But if I hold a grudge toward them, does that
mean God won't forgive my sins? This is scary stuff.

Then I think, *Wait a minute. This sounds like a cosmic tit-for-tat.*
"You forgive others," we imagine God saying, "and then I'll forgive you. Otherwise, we have no deal." This sounds just the opposite of the God I know who is merciful and gracious—He does not
give us the punishment we deserve but rather the grace we do not
deserve. So what did Jesus mean?

Jesus meant that if we refuse to forgive—if we become consumed with bitterness and resentment toward someone—we so

harden ourselves that we cut ourselves off from our relationship with God. If we are unwilling to forgive people who have hurt us, it is not that God refuses to forgive us but that we allow our hearts to become so hardened that we will not come to God and ask Him for forgiveness, we will not come to Him for mercy—we will not come to Him for anything else for that matter.

Jesus illustrated this principle in the parable of the Pharisee and the publican:

> Two men went up to the temple to pray, one a Pharisee and the other a tax collector. The Pharisee stood up and prayed about himself. "God, I thank you that I am not like other men—robbers, evildoers, adulterers—or even like this tax collector" (Luke 18:10-11).

The Pharisee started his prayer well enough, but his prayer rapidly deteriorated. He thanked God, which was good; but he shifted his focus from where it ought to be, on God, to where it shouldn't be, on others.

Then the Pharisee continued, "I fast twice a week and give a tenth of all I get" (Luke 18:12). The Law only proscribed one day of fasting for the Jewish people, the Day of Atonement; but the Pharisee boasted that he fasted well beyond the call of duty and congratulated himself that he tithed on all he earned. Rather than thanking God for all his gifts, he let God know there are things for which *God should thank him*. He did not bring himself to God at all. He didn't praise God. He made no confession. He didn't ask God for anything. He did not really pray to God at all. He just told God what a wonderful person he was.

The publican, or tax collector, was quite different: "He would not even look up to heaven, but beat his breast and said,

'God, have mercy on me, a sinner' " (Luke 18:13). The tax collector was overwhelmed by how far from God he felt because he knew that he had sinned. He felt so distant from God that he wouldn't even lift his eyes. He simply asked God for mercy.

Jesus concluded the parable by saying, "I tell you that this man, rather than the other, went home justified before God. For everyone who exalts himself will be humbled, and he who humbles himself will be exalted" (Luke 18:14).

The Pharisee despised the publican and others like him. In fact, he thanked God that he was not sinful like the tax collector. He was so confident in his own righteousness that he didn't think he needed forgiveness and didn't really come before God at all.

It is only when we view ourselves like the tax collector, when we have a sense of unworthiness due to our sins, that we will be likely to come to God for forgiveness. Forgiveness of others, then, is not something we do in order to be forgiven. It is something we do because we are aware of how much we have already been forgiven. Because we have been forgiven much, we want to forgive much. Let me give you a relatively modern example of this principle in play.

On February 17, 1985, some 400 men and women gathered to pray in St. Patrick's Church, in Canonsburg, Pennsylvania. The McGraw-Edison Company had told its employees that without a considerable giveback in wages and benefits, the company would close down its Canonsburg plant; but the union leadership had refused to do so. If the plant closed, the impact on the town would be disastrous; so Rev. David Kinsey, chairman of the Canonsburg Ministerial Association, along with the ministers of the town, the McGraw-Edison labor and management personnel and their families, and a large ecumenical group of praying people, gathered to ask God to change hearts and change history.

At the climax of that prayer rally, Wayne T. Alderson, a Christian labor relations and management consultant and founder of Value of the Person Inc., called the senior management representative for McGraw-Edison and the president of the local United Steel Workers Union to come and pray with him at the front of the church. The labor leader prayed for McGraw-Edison management, and the manager prayed for the trade union leaders and membership. The result? Two days later, management changed its offer (though there was still to be a reduction in salary and benefits) and the labor force changed its vote, and the plant remained open.

THE DARE

Today I would like you to do some self-examination. Is there someone you need to forgive? Choosing to forgive that person does not mean you will have full reconciliation in your relationship. However, it does mean that you will be choosing to step out of the dungeon of bitterness and that you will be as gracious to that person as God has been gracious with you.

The first part of your dare today is to forgive someone who has hurt you. Forgiving others will help your relationship with God. It will help you see more clearly to ask God to forgive you.

What are the names of some of the people you need to forgive?
Ask God to help you do so.

_____

_____

_____

_____

_____

The second part of your dare is to see if God brings anything to
light for which you need to ask His forgiveness. What sins do
you need to confess? If you are willing, write those sins down
right now.

_____

_____

_____

_____

_____

Pray with Humility

*Lord, don't trouble yourself, for I do not deserve to have
you come under my roof. That is why I did not consider
myself worthy to come to you.*
LUKE 7:6-7

Luke tells us that a centurion, an officer in the Roman army
who evidently served under Herod Antipas, tetrarch of Galilee
and Perea, had a servant who suffered from a form of paralysis
that involved extreme pain. Physicians had been unable to help
him. He sent some Jewish leaders in the synagogue to ask Jesus
to come heal his servant. The centurion probably worked at the
Roman garrison of Capernaum. He was a Gentile by birth but
apparently was one of many Gentiles who were at the time
deeply feeling the emptiness and falsehood of all the polythe-
istic religions in the first century. They were attracted to the
monotheism of the Jewish faith. He had probably heard Jesus
teach, and more than likely knew people who had been healed
by Jesus, so he was convinced Jesus could heal his servant.

According to Luke's account, the centurion did not come
himself. Instead, he contacted the Jewish authorities to see if
they would bring his request to Jesus. Luke tells us:

The centurion heard of Jesus and sent some elders of the
Jews to him, asking him to come and heal his servant.

When they came to Jesus, they pleaded earnestly with him, "This man deserves to have you do this, because he loves our nation and has built our synagogue." So Jesus went with them (Luke 7:3-6).

I surmise that the centurion was a Jewish proselyte who had given a significant amount of money to build the Capernaum synagogue. Luke suggests that he built the whole thing. He had a good relationship with the leaders of the synagogue, so he asked them if they would approach Jesus on his behalf. So the Jewish leaders put in a good word for him, letting Jesus know that he deserved anything Jesus could do for him.

He was not far from the house when the centurion sent friends to say to him: "Lord, don't trouble yourself, for I do not deserve to have you come under my roof. That is why I did not consider myself worthy to come to you" (Luke 7:6-7).

The centurion didn't feel worthy to come to Jesus, so he sent others to implore Christ on his behalf. When Jesus was part way there, he sent other people to tell Jesus he wasn't worthy to even have Jesus come to his home. He did not come with a demanding faith. He didn't come with the attitude, "Hey, I'm a centurion. Everybody around here knows I'm a pretty important person and I gave a lot of money to get the synagogue in Capernaum built. After all I've done, you owe me one, Jesus." Rather, he came with humility.

Effective prayer is marked by humility. We humbly admit to God that we've sinned, done a lot of stupid things, and don't deserve anything from Him.

A couple years ago, we had four sons who drive living with us, one with his wife and one with a girlfriend who was at our house frequently. That meant that some nights, counting my wife's car and my car, we had eight cars parked at our house. To avoid costly driveway accidents, I asked that none of them park outside the three bays of our garage, but even with this dictum in place, it still was wise for those with cars parked in the garage to look to see if a car was parked behind them before backing out of the garage. It would be foolish to back out in faith that everyone abided by the dictum to not park outside the garage bays.

One day, one of us did just that. They backed out without looking and slammed into our oldest son's car, causing a lot of foolish and expensive damage. I won't mention who did this stupid thing. I don't want to embarrass them in this book. But I will tell you it wasn't my wife, Jorie, it wasn't one of our sons, it wasn't our daughter-in-law, and it wasn't our son's girlfriend. One day I jumped in my car, hit the garage door opener, backed out without looking, and bam! I couldn't believe it. For a Scottish guy like me, who is always looking for ways to save money, that was a disaster.

We have to humbly admit the stupid things we do. We have to humbly admit our mistakes and sins. We can't come with the attitude: "After all I've done for you, God, you owe me one." That will never work.

THE DARE

Today I want you to not only confess your sins, but also admit that God doesn't owe you anything. You're not coming to collect your reward. You're coming for mercy.

What are the reasons why God doesn't owe you anything? Write these out below.

_____

_____

_____

_____

_____

How does it feel to admit that God doesn't owe you anything? How does it feel to know that you can only ask for His mercy and grace?

_____

_____

_____

_____

_____

19

Obey God

If you remain in me and my words remain in you,
ask whatever you wish, and it will be given you.
JOHN 15:7

My wife and I have nine children: five sons and four daughters. Some people think we're crazy, but we love it. Many people ask us how we do it. We have found that in order to make it, we have to be organized. To that end, over the years, we have given our kids certain jobs for which they are responsible. If each one does his or her part, we do all right. But if one of us drops the ball, we struggle.

One day before I left for work, I asked our son who was responsible for the yard to mow the lawn, clean his room and get his stuff that was clogging up the entryway picked up and put away in his room before I got home that night. That evening as I drove up to our house, I noticed that the lawn looked even shaggier than it had in the morning. I opened the door to the house and saw my son's backpack, tennis bag, coat, shoes and clothes still strewn all over the floor. I walked into the kitchen and found the sports page scattered across the counter and around a half-eaten bowl of cereal. A cereal box, with its top open wide, lay nearby on its side, next to a half-full jug of milk, now room temperature. The toaster sat out, along with a tub of margarine stabbed with a knife and sprinkled with crumbs. A jar of jam sat open next to a knife covered with sticky preserves, nearly glued to the granite counter. A banana peel lay sprawled next to orange peels that were scattered over the counter. A half-used loaf of bread lay open next to a package of lunchmeat. A knife stuck out of a nearly full jar of mayonnaise. I could trace nearly every move my son had made that day.

Thoroughly irritated, I marched upstairs and knocked on his door. "Come on in!" he yelled above the beat of the music vibrating from his room. I pushed the door open slowly, no small feat with all the crumpled clothes wedged behind the door.

Let me ask you: Do you think this was a good time for him to ask me if he could use the car? Or do you think he had some explaining to do before asking me for anything?

In much the same way, some of us have some explaining to do before asking any favors of God.

Jesus said, "If you remain in me and my words remain in you, ask whatever you wish, and it will be given you" (John 15:7). What a promise. Ask whatever you want and it will be done for you. But there's a condition. You must remain in Him and have His words remain in you. That means you have to spend time with Christ in His Word. How else would His words remain in you? You have to stay close to Him, doing what He asks of you. When we disobey, we separate ourselves from Him. Christ says God will take us seriously, if we take Him seriously. He'll do what we ask, if we do what He asks.

John says much the same thing: "We receive from him anything we ask, because we obey his commands and do what pleases him" (1 John 3:22). Obedience is essential to effective and powerful prayers.

When our prayers are not answered, we're prone to wonder, *What's wrong with God? Why won't He give me a break?* Not many people are willing to take an honest look inside and admit, *Maybe I'm the problem*. If your prayers are not being answered, maybe it's time for you to take a long look inside to see if you're the problem.

All five of our sons have played competitive tennis. They played in tournaments around the Pacific Northwest and participated in high school tennis. Three of them also played in national tournaments. Involvement at that level required lessons, team practices, matches and conditioning. Every day Jorie or I drove them to their practices.

One day it was my turn to drive. Before I left for work, I told the boys that I would be back at such and such a time to pick them up. I told them to make sure they were fed and had all their gear packed, so they were ready to go. I arrived home at the prescribed time. I don't know what I was thinking, but for some reason I assumed that when I rang the doorbell, they would all be standing at attention with their tennis bags slung over their shoulders. Instead, I found all of them in disarray. They weren't dressed, they hadn't eaten, and they didn't have their stuff ready to go.

I was instantly irked. I said, "Let's go, guys. Hurry up or you're going to be late," with a sharp tone to my voice. But in spite of my best efforts to herd them out the door, minutes kept ticking by. Finally, in frustration, I walked out and sat in the car parked in the driveway outside the garage to wait for them. I waited . . . and I waited. One at a time they straggled out, usually with a sandwich in one hand, shoes and clothes in another, and a tennis bag slung over a shoulder. The longer I had to wait, the angrier I became. I thought, *How can they be so disorganized and so inconsiderate of my valuable time?*

By the time the last one straggled out and into the car, I was so upset, I punched the accelerator, assuming it was in reverse.

It wasn't. The car lurched forward, slamming into the garage, creating a one-foot gash. The boys sat in stunned silence as I backed up and drove them, without speaking, to their practice.

About halfway there, I was feeling so humiliated by what I had done that I said, "Boys, I'm sorry for getting angry with you. I'm sorry for yelling at you, and I'm sorry for getting so upset with you that I exhibited some stupid driveway rage. It wasn't what Jesus would do. Would you please forgive me?" Then I prayed and asked God to forgive me.

I knew I couldn't have a healthy relationship with my sons if I didn't confess my sin. And I knew there was no way I could have an open relationship with God and ask Him for anything until I had cleared this matter up with Him. I couldn't expect God to grant my requests, when I wasn't living in obedience.

There's a sequel to that story. The following Sunday, I confessed my angry outburst to my congregation. The week after that, I saw no less than a half dozen parishioners drive slowly by our house, inspecting the devastation to the garage. It's possible that they just wanted to see what a sinner they had for a pastor; I hope the reason was that they wanted evidence that examples in my sermons weren't fiction and that their pastor, like them, was certainly capable of making mistakes.

If we want to see answers to our prayers, we need to obey.

THE DARE

Today, I want you to face up to any disobedience against God that is in your life. Is there anything God has asked you to do that you have not done? Is there an area in your life

where you know you are living in disobedience to God? Please write those things down now.

_____

_____

_____

_____

_____

Read Jesus' words in John 15:7 one more time: "If you remain in me and my words remain in you, ask whatever you wish, and it will be given you." What does that mean to you? Using totally different words, write out what it would mean for you to fulfill this verse.

_____

_____

_____

_____

_____

20

Pray for God's Glory

Now, O LORD our God, deliver us from his hand, so that all the kingdoms on earth may know that you alone, O LORD, are God.

2 KINGS 19:19

During the first eight months of 1981, Sunset Presbyterian Church had an average of only 25 people in worship each Sunday. Desperate and not knowing what to do, the leaders of the church discussed shutting their doors and calling it quits. Then in one last gasp, they decided to call me as their new pastor. (I told you they were desperate.) Jorie and I decided God was behind this call, so we agreed to move.

When I accepted, I discovered that when the church had needed help to pay their bills, they had rented out the classroom portion of their building to a strong, non-Christian preschool that had over 100 preschoolers in attendance. I thought that was wonderful. We were trying to tell people about Jesus, and here were 100 families in our building five days a week.

The church and the preschool had a great relationship in the early days. A number of the families from the preschool began to attend our church. As our church began to grow and establish a Sunday School, however, we began to need the space that in previous years had been rented to the preschool. With God's help, a lot of prayer and a lot of hard work, the church began to steadily grow; and within nine months, we had over 200 people attending worship on Sundays. The preschool staff was not used to sharing space with an active and growing congregation, and none of our church leaders had ever taken a course in how to manage tenants. As we began to reassert ownership over our classrooms, conflicts arose.

For example, our Sunday School teachers began to complain that the preschool staff was stealing our supplies. The preschool staff lodged similar charges against our staff. The preschool requested that before we went home on Sundays, we turn our pictures of Jesus around, and remove any Bible verses or Christian symbols from the walls. These requests didn't go over well with our teachers. Our people thought, *Wait a minute. Don't we own these buildings?*

So we set down some new guidelines for the amount of space the preschool was allowed to use and what the preschool could and could not do in our classrooms. The preschool staff was not happy with the new rules, and they began to spread the word to their families that we were being quite unfair with them. Since I was the primary person with whom they interacted, defamatory remarks about me also started to make the rounds. When tensions reached a boiling point, our session decided that the sharing of space was no longer workable. We told the preschool that we would not continue to rent space to them the next fall—they would need to find a new home. It's probably needless to say that when we delivered the news, they became angry. Since I was the face of the church to them, they began to circulate reports that the new pastor was treating them horribly. I became like the new Joseph Stalin in the preschool community.

I remember praying, "Lord, I don't care what they say about me. And I'm not concerned with what is said about our church session. But, Lord, stop these rumors that are so untrue, lest

Your name be dragged through the mud and people be lost from Your Kingdom who we otherwise might reach."

If you want your prayers answered, don't make requests for your reputation. Pray for things that increase God's reputation.

That's what Hezekiah, when he was the king of Judah, did when the king of Assyria, the most powerful man in the world at the time, sent his army to attack Jerusalem. The commander of the Assyrian army boasted that he had defeated all the nations around Judah and was going to do the same thing to Jerusalem. He told the people of Judah not to believe Hezekiah when he told them that the God of Israel would protect them: "Has the god of any nation ever delivered his land from the hand of the king of Assyria?" (2 Kings 18:33). He told Hezekiah to surrender, or he and his people would all be destroyed.

In response, Hezekiah prayed:

> Give ear, O LORD, and hear; open your eyes, O LORD, and see; listen to the words Sennacherib has sent to insult the living God. It is true, O LORD, that the Assyrian kings have laid waste these nations and their lands, they have thrown their gods into the fire and destroyed them, for they were not gods but only wood and stone, fashioned by men's hands. Now, O LORD our God, deliver us from his hand, so that all kingdoms on earth may know that you alone, O LORD, are God (2 Kings 19:16-19).

Hezekiah did not pray for God to deliver him so that his popularity ratings would go up and the people would continue to support him as monarch. He prayed for God to intervene so that all the kingdoms on earth would know that He alone was

God. He prayed, "Lord, Sennacherib is making a mockery of you. He is claiming You cannot protect us and that You are no stronger than the other dead gods he has destroyed. He's saying You are no different from any other gods. God, Your reputation is at stake here! God, vindicate Your name! Show Your power! Deliver us so that people may know that You are God." That's powerful praying. That's praying with the proper motive. It's praying for God's glory. (And, of course, God defeated the king of Assyria and his army!)

If you want to pray with power, ask for things that bring God glory. Don't ask for *your* glory but for *His* glory. Your top concern must be to bring honor to God.

Win victory by praying like Hezekiah did.

THE DARE

Today, I want you to treat your prayer requests differently. Start with praise and confession, as usual, but when you get to requests, word them in such a way that they bring glory to God. An example would be to ask God to help you treat your spouse or children with love, not so that they will think you are wonderful, but so they will give thanks to God for giving them a good husband or father.

What are your prayer requests?

_____

_____

_____

_____

_____

_____

Now look back through your record of answers to prayers. How did the answers bring glory to God?

_____

_____

_____

_____

_____

21

Be Specific and Go Public

*Be strong and courageous. Do not be afraid or discouraged because
of the king of Assyria and the vast army with him, for there is a greater
power with us than with him. With him is only the arm of flesh,
but with us is the LORD our God to help us and to fight our battles.*
2 CHRONICLES 32:7-8

When Jorie and I first met, we worked together with high school
students. Before one of our weekend trips, Jorie sat down with a
high school girl she discipled and asked, "Marcia, how many
sophomore girls would you like to see come on the weekend?
How many girls should we ask God to help us get on this retreat?"

Marcia thought for a minute and said, "Let's pray for 12."
So they asked God for 12. They prayed. They talked to girls. They
prayed some more. They made calls. As the retreat began, Jorie
and Marcia spent a rare moment alone in their cabin. Marcia
said to Jorie, "Do you know how many sophomore girls we have
in our cabin?" They counted the sleeping bags in the room. Sure
enough, with God's help they had gotten 12 girls to come. Marcia was so excited. Because they were specific in asking for 12, it
was pretty obvious that God had answered their prayers.

I believe God is more inclined to answer our prayers when
we make specific requests of Him. Think about it. If we ask God
to bless us, how are we going to know if He did? If we ask
God for something general (take care of all the orphan children

in the world), how will we know if He did? But if we ask God to help us in some specific way (provide this month's supply of food for the Church Street Orphanage), it is more obvious when He answers our prayers. And when it is clear that God has answered our prayers, we are more inclined to give Him the glory. (And remember, God answers prayers that bring Him glory.) So make your requests of God specific.

Our prayers are also more powerful when we go public with them. Jorie and Marcia stated publicly to one another that they were asking God for 12 girls. If God did not answer their prayers, they faced the possibility of being embarrassed. God was pleased to answer their request, because they had taken the risk of going public with it.

We see this prayer principle of being specific and going public in Hezekiah's prayer to God when the king of Assyria and his army threatened Jerusalem (the prayer we looked at in the previous chapter).

What did Hezekiah do? "Hezekiah received the letter from the messengers [demanding their surrender] and read it. Then he went up to the temple of the LORD and spread it out before the LORD. And Hezekiah prayed to the Lord" (2 Kings 19:14). And in his prayer, Hezekiah made a specific request of God; Deliver Jerusalem from the Assyrian army. It was a specific request so that it would be quite obvious if God answered.

Not only was Hezekiah specific, but he also went public with his prayer. He told the people of Judah what he had prayed. He told them he had asked God to deliver them and that he believed God was going to do just that:

> Be strong and courageous. Do not be afraid or discouraged because of the king of Assyria and the vast army

with him, for there is a greater power with us than with him. With him is only the arm of flesh, but with us is the LORD our God to help us and to fight our battles (2 Chron. 32:7-8).

It took a lot of courage for Hezekiah to tell the people that he was confident that God would deliver them from the Assyrians. He risked having himself and his people slaughtered. Yet it was precisely because of his unabashed public faith in God that the Lord answered his prayer.

God loves when we go out on a limb for Him. Going public with specific requests we have made of God increases our risk, but it also increases power in our prayers.

THE DARE

Today's challenge is for you to be both specific and public in your prayers. First, I would like you to make your requests specific. Make them specific enough so that by days' end you can evaluate whether or not God answered your prayers. Then, I want you to take the risk of going public with some of your requests. You can do this by praying with someone else so that they hear what you are asking of God or by telling someone what you have asked of God and believe He is going to do.

As you do this, you are entering into my world and the whole reason I wrote this book. For years I have made it my practice to make specific requests of God and to frequently go public with some of them. The next morning, I think about the previous day and record answers to prayer. This daily practice has caused me to grow so much in my faith that I wanted to share this with you.

What specific requests are you making of God today? Write these below.

_____

_____

_____

_____

_____

At the end of the day or the next morning, think back through your day. What answers have you seen to specific requests you made of God?

_____

_____

_____

_____

_____

Were you able to publicly announce one of your specific prayer requests? Or did you pray aloud with anyone? Please write your experience below.

_____

_____

_____

_____

_____

22

Pray God's Promises

Remember the instruction you gave your servant Moses, saying,
If you are unfaithful, I will scatter you among the nations, but if you
return to me and obey my commands, then even if your exiled people
are at the farthest horizon, I will gather them from there and bring
them to the place I have chosen as a dwelling for my Name.
NEHEMIAH 1:8-9

The book of Nehemiah opens when Nehemiah was one of the Jewish exiles living in Susa, one of the capitals of the Persian Empire. Nehemiah's brother and some buddies had just returned from a trip to Jerusalem. Nehemiah asked about the welfare of the Jews who had returned to Judah, and Nehemiah learned the upsetting news that the city gates and the protective walls of the city had been torn down and lay in rubble.

So what did Nehemiah do? He prayed. He realized that to have the walls of the capital city of God's people in rubble was an embarrassment to God's name. He prayed that God would enable him to go and rebuild the walls. What I want you to notice about Nehemiah's prayer is how he claimed God's promise that if the Jews returned to Him and obeyed His commands, He would restore them:

Remember the instruction you gave your servant Moses, saying, "If you are unfaithful, I will scatter you among the nations, but if you return to me and obey my commands, then even if your exiled people are at the farthest horizon, I will gather them from there and bring them to the place I have chosen as a dwelling for my Name" (Neh. 1:8-9).

Nehemiah reminded God of His promise to Moses: "If you disobey Me, I will scatter you, but after you are scattered, if you return to Me, I will restore you again to Jerusalem" (see Deut. 29:25-28; 30:1-5). (Technically, of course, we don't remind God of anything. He's omniscient. It's probably more accurate to say we remind ourselves of what God has promised. But Scriptures teach us that God loves for us to remind Him of His promises and pray them back to Him. A schoolteacher loves when students write principles she has taught during the year back to her on the test paper. Likewise God loves to see us remember His promises.)

In the rest of his prayer, Nehemiah basically said, "Lord, You fulfilled the first part. We're scattered. Now we're ready to take You seriously again, so restore us to the land. Take me back to Jerusalem, so I can rebuild the walls." And God granted Nehemiah's request.

In Exodus, Moses had prayed much the same way as Nehemiah did. When the people of Israel molded a golden idol in the shape of a calf and were dancing before it, God told Moses He wanted to destroy the people. Moses pleaded with God on behalf of the people. He reminded God of His promise:

Turn from your fierce anger; relent and do not bring disaster on your people. Remember your servants Abraham, Isaac and Israel, to whom you swore by your own self: "I will make your descendants as numerous as the stars in the sky and I will give your descendants all this land I promised them, and it will be their inheritance forever." Then the LORD relented and did not bring on his people the disaster he had threatened (Exod. 32:12-14).

Moses essentially said, "God, You can't fulfill Your promise if You destroy Your people."

Do you see how important this is? When we pray for that which God has promised to give, we are assured of receiving what we request, because we are asking for something God has already promised to grant.

My wife grew up in Chicago, and her family had a lake house on Lake Michigan where they went every summer. Behind their house was a little lake stocked with fish that froze over every winter. Suppose your friend suggests that you go ice fishing on that lake. You try it, but you don't catch anything, because you are afraid to walk out onto the middle of it for fear that the ice will break. Your friend has fished on ice before. He walks out onto the middle of the lake, sits on a box, chips a hole, begins to fish and catches gobs of fish. Is the ice any stronger for him than for you? No. The difference is that he knows ice and he knows where he can walk on it with confidence.

It's the same with prayer. Why do some believers pray with more confidence and authority than others? Because they know what God has promised to give us. They know what promises to claim. What are some of the things God has promised to give us if we ask?

- He promises that if we put His kingdom first, He will meet all our needs (see Matt. 6:33).

- He promises to build His church and that the gates of hell will not prevail against it (see Matt. 16:18).

- He promises us authority over the spiritual forces of evil (see Luke 10:17).

- He promises eternal life to those who believe (see John 3:16).

- He promises a way of escape when we are tempted (see 1 Cor. 10:13).

- He promises that husbands who love their wives will be glad they do, for to love your wife is to love yourself (see Eph. 5:28).

- He promises that it will go well for children who obey their parents (see Eph. 6:1-3).

- He promises to meet all our needs (see Phil. 4:19).

- He promises to give us wisdom when we need guidance (see Jas. 1:2-4).

- He promises that if we resist the devil, he will flee from us (see Jas. 4:7).

When we pray for these things, we have assurance we will receive them, for God has promised to grant these requests.

When our kids have a birthday, I try to take them out for lunch. Once, for various reasons, I did not take one of our daughters out on her special day or even within a few days of it. She eventually asked me, "Daddy, are you still going to take me out for my birthday lunch?" I said, "Honey, of course I am. I've got it scheduled for next Saturday. I wouldn't think of not fulfilling my promise to take you out for lunch."

If human parents keep their promises to their kids, how much more do you think our heavenly Father will keep His promises to us, *His* children?

THE DARE

Today, I would like you to pray for something that God has promised to give. Or, to put it another way, whatever you have requested God to do, find a promise of God that assures you God is happy to grant your request. Of course, to pray God's promises, you have to know them. So I would like you to make a list of things that God has promised in the Bible. As you read the Bible in the days ahead, look for promises of God that you can add to this list.

_____

_____

_____

_____

_____

What are some requests you have of God? Write these down, and then next to it put a promise of God that assures you He would be happy to grant your request.

_____

_____

_____

_____

_____

23

Pray with Others

Again, I tell you that if two of you on earth agree about anything
you ask for, it will be done for you by my Father in heaven. For where
two or three come together in my name, there am I with them.
MATTHEW 18:19-20

God has blessed Jorie and me with great kids. All nine of our children committed their lives to Christ at very young ages. But we have had some challenges.

When one of our sons was going into tenth grade, our family moved to a new house, so he began attending a different high school. There he made a whole new group of friends and started making some bad choices; and the wonderful, sensitive and kind son we had known for 15 years almost overnight turned into a difficult and surly son.

Our son already liked to live on the edge. He had a penchant for doing dangerous things. He loved to hike, but when he did, he chose the most dangerous trails. One day, he announced he was going skydiving with a friend.

The most dangerous thing that I was aware that he did was with his Young Life leader. We loved and trusted this leader, but he was wild and crazy, too. He would take high school guys to the auto auction and pick up old cars for $50. Then they would go high up into the hills and drive these beaters off-road until they totally destroyed them. Our son showed us pictures of one of these cars. They had painted "Death Box!" in big letters on the back of it

During these years, our son neglected his studies, so his grades went south. He started drinking a bit and staying out late past his curfew. He resisted our attempts to rein him in, so our relationship became contentious. Many nights we went to bed worried sick because he was still not home. My worst nightmare, which I had more than a few times, was being awakened late at night by a call from the police informing us that they had our son down at the police station, or that they had found our son on the side of the road in a car accident.

We prayed about him all the time. What helped the most during those years was a wonderful group of friends with whom we could share our concerns. We told the members of our care group what was going on, and they prayed with us. In fact, they prayed for our son for years. I don't know how we would have made it without these friends and their prayers.

After our son graduated from high school and realized he was not doing well in college, he decided to join Youth With A Mission for a year. With that group, he started to study the Bible, went out on missions to various countries and became a different man. This turnaround in our son, we believe, was in good part due to the prayers of our friends.

There is more power available to us when we pray with other believers. That's why Jesus said, "Again, I tell you that if two of you on earth agree about anything you ask for, it will be done for you by my Father in heaven. For where two or three come together in my name, there am I with them" (Matt. 18:19-20). It's not enough, notice, to just pray with other believers. We need to agree with them about what we are asking for—

we all must be praying for the same thing. Then, Jesus promised, our prayers are powerful.

This is what the early believers did when Peter and John were thrown in jail. They prayed with unanimous agreement that the message of Jesus Christ must go forward in the face of threats from the religious establishment, and God demonstrated His pleasure with their prayer by shaking the building and filling the believers with the Holy Spirit (see chapter 15 for a detailed discussion of this incident).

Even earlier, the disciples made a habit of gathering together to pray together: "They all joined together constantly in prayer, along with the women and Mary the mother of Jesus, and with his brothers" (Acts 1:14). Later, corporate prayers for Peter when he was in prison resulted in his release (see Acts 12:1-11). Paul knew the value of corporate prayer, and he did not think twice about asking for it when in need:

> I urge you, brothers, by our Lord Jesus Christ and by the love of the Spirit, to join me in my struggle by praying to God for me. Pray that I may be rescued from the unbelievers in Judea and that my service in Jerusalem may be acceptable to the saints there (Rom. 15:30-31).

> Pray also for me, that whenever I open my mouth, words may be given me so that I will fearlessly make known the mystery of the gospel, for which I am an ambassador in chains. Pray that I may declare it fearlessly, as I should (Eph. 6:19-20).

In fact, Paul assumed corporate prayer would bring about whatever was necessary:

On [God] we have set our hope that he will continue to deliver us, as you help us by your prayers. Then many will give thanks on our behalf for the gracious favor granted us in answer to the prayers of many (2 Cor. 1:10-11).

The power and value of praying with other believers is inestimable. Whatever your situation—single, married to an unpraying spouse, no home church—I want you to begin the search for prayer partners. If you're married and have a believing spouse, ask your mate to pray with you. If you have children, begin praying with them. Ask a friend to pray with you. Find a church if you don't have one. Seek out a small group of people with whom you can pray. And if you think that you're too busy to do this, remember that you have too many big things at stake in your life to not be praying with other believers.

THE DARE

Most of the dares so far have been about you praying alone. Today, I again want you to pray with someone else. Whatever your situation, I want you to begin the search for prayer partners.

What are the names of some people who you could ask to pray with you? What time could you all get together?

_____

_____

_____

_____

_____

_____

When you get together with your partner or group, what subjects could you pray about, one at a time? (It's a good idea to pray about one subject at a time, maybe each person praying from a different perspective so that there is agreement on what all participants believe is God's will.)

_____

_____

_____

_____

_____

_____

_____

24

Align Your Will

This is the confidence we have in approaching God: that if we ask anything according to his will, he hears us. And if we know that he hears us—whatever we ask—we know that we have what we asked of him.
1 JOHN 5:14-15

I do not give my children all the things they request of me. If I did, I would not be a good father. So why do we expect God to give us everything we ask of Him?

When our fifth son was four, on many mornings he and I would shave together. He would run into my bathroom and ask, "Are we going to shave, Daddy?"

I would reply, "How old are you?"

"Four," he smiled with an impish grin.

"Four! And you're already shaving? Most boys don't shave until they're 16! Are you sure you need a shave? Is your beard long and hairy?"

"Yes," he laughed, repeating this conversation he'd had with me many times before.

So I put a little extra shaving cream in my hand so there would be enough for him when I finished lathering my face. He never failed to giggle with delight when I put the extra shaving cream in his hand. He proceeded to wipe it all over his face, sometimes even on his ears. Then while I shaved, he danced in front of the mirror with his lathered face.

Did I give him a razor blade if he requested it? No. I would have been a negligent parent if I granted such a request. I don't give any of my children things with which they can hurt themselves. No parent gives a young child a sharp knife or a loaded gun or allows him or her to play in the medicine chest.

In the same way, God does not grant requests that He knows will not be good for us. He does not give us things that are not in His will, something that He knows we will be better off without. So why do we complain when He withholds something from us? If it had been good for us, He would have given it to us. We make many requests that, from His perspective, are dangerous or harmful for us. So His answer is no.

In one of the most amazing promises concerning prayer in the Bible, John said, "This is the confidence we have in approaching God: that if we ask anything according to his will, he hears us. And if we know that he hears us—whatever we ask—we know that we have what we asked of him" (1 John 5:14-15). The key to receiving answers to our prayers is to pray for things that are in God's will. God promises that if we make requests that align with His will, He will happily grant them.

Some people complain that if you end your prayer with the disclaimer "Grant this, if it is Your will, God," all the power is taken out of praying—as if you pour out your heart to God and then say, "But if this isn't in Your will, then forget I even brought it up." I, however, don't think this is a bad way to end a prayer. There are a lot of things we can be certain are in God's will, but there *are* times when we can't be totally certain if what we are requesting is in God's will. It may appear to us that what we ask for will bring God glory, but we may be unaware that there may be another way that brings Him more glory. In such cases, it's better to admit to God that we don't know what is best: "Lord, here is a request I am not quite sure about. It looks good to me; but, Lord, don't give it to me if it's not in Your will."

A person in our church woke up one day with severe bronchitis. It got so bad that she couldn't breathe, so she went to the hospital. While in the emergency room, she had a heart attack. They gave her a stress test, which indicated she had a blockage, so they decided to perform an angiogram to determine exactly where the blockage was.

While lying on the table waiting for the angiogram to begin, she prayed, "God, I really like my life. I want to enjoy many more years with my husband and family. However, if it is Your will to take me home, I want You to know that obeying You is more important to me than living. So, Lord, if You want me with You, I am ready to go."

After she prayed that prayer, she said a peace settled over her like a warm blanket. She felt as if she were floating in the wonderful, warm cocoon of God's arms. She knew that whatever happened, she was in God's hands.

When you say to God, "Lord, I want Your will, not mine," and then pray for what you believe is in God's will, that's good praying. If the only things you want are things that God wants, you have the assurance that your prayers—whatever they are—will be answered. Wow!

THE DARE

If you and I had to pick one dare out of this book that is the most important one of all, this one might be it. This one contains the key to knowing that your prayers will be answered. So as you pray today, I want you to think carefully about whether or not what you are asking is in God's will. If you are not certain it is in God's will, ask Him to help you change the request so that it is in His will.

Write down your requests today. Why do you believe each request is in God's will? Write your answer after each request.

Review some of your past requests. Why do you think they may not have been in God's will?

25

Pray with Faith

"Say the word, and my servant will be healed."... When Jesus heard
this, he was amazed at him, and turning to the crowd following him,
he said, "I tell you, I have not found such great faith even in Israel."
LUKE 7:6-9

A couple years ago, Jorie and I took our 12-year-old daughter to
the Girls 12s Winter Nationals Tennis Tournament in Tucson,
Arizona. As we boarded the plane to return to Portland with her,
our 9-year-old and our 6-year-old, the agent wrote down the girls'
names, and said, "We have to be very careful to get all the children's names when we have weather like this." Neither of us had
checked the weather report, so we had no idea what the agent
was talking about. I wasn't too worried about it, because I knew
that if the flight hadn't been cancelled, flying had been deemed
safe. I just figured that there was rough weather somewhere in
Arizona and that we didn't have anything to worry about.

As it turned out, there were 60-mph gusts of wind in Portland. And sure enough, when we made our approach into Portland, things got really rough. A couple times the plane made
sudden drops in altitude, and occasionally, the wings seemed to
flail up and down. I assumed that once we got through the
clouds, there would be no more turbulence, but it continued
all the way to the ground. At first, the plane was bouncing
around so badly, I began to wonder if we were going to make it.

I squeezed Jorie's hand tighter. I prayed, "Lord, put an angel under this plane!"

I prayed, but I wasn't sure if my prayer would be answered. As we neared the runway, the plane swayed back and forth so badly, the wing almost hit the runway. I was never so relieved as when the pilot got the plane down on the runway. Things had been so bad that after we landed a full-grown man in the seat behind us assumed a sort-of crash position (he put his knees on the seat cushion and buried his head in the top of the seat-back cushion) and took deep breaths for a full five minutes.

Have you ever been in a situation where you prayed, but you lacked faith and didn't really believe that God was going to answer your prayer? Maybe you prayed for a good grade in a class, but you didn't really believe you were going to do well. Maybe you pleaded with God to help you find a job, but you doubted it would actually happen. Maybe you prayed for healing but didn't expect to get well.

God is looking for people who put their complete faith in Him, for people who pray with faith, for people who impress Him with their complete trust in Him.

The centurion described in Luke 7 is one person in the Bible who impressed God in just this way. Through emissaries, the centurion said to Jesus:

> Say the word, and my servant will be healed. . . . When Jesus heard this, he was amazed at him, and turning to the crowd following him, he said, "I tell you, I have not found such great faith even in Israel" (Luke 7:7-9).

The centurion had complete confidence that Jesus not only had the ability but also had the willingness to act on his be-

half. Astounded and impressed by this show of faith, Jesus healed the servant without ever seeing him (for a discussion of the humility exhibited by the centurion in this situation, see chapter 18).

A number of years ago I was asked to speak for a second time at Young Life's camp in Malibu, Canada. As I had before, I took Jorie and our four oldest boys with me. The boys were excited to go because they all looked forward to having a second try at learning how to water ski. The year before they had tried to ski but had not been successful. (It had been cool that week and the water temperature was somewhere in the upper 50s. After a few tries, the boys got so cold that they gave up.)

This time David, my second son, asked, "Dad, can we get a wet suit?"

I said, "David, I'm sorry, but we can't afford a wet suit."

He replied, "Well, can you borrow one from one of your friends?" He knew I water skied and had friends with wet suits and dry suits.

I said, "David, I'm not going to ask one of my friends. But how about if you pray and ask God to provide one for you." I thought praying for the wet suit would be a good exercise in faith for David.

So David began to pray. Nearly every night, when we said our prayers, David asked God to provide him with a wet suit.

When we arrived in Malibu, we were shown to our cabin, and shortly, Jorie came out laughing. She said to me, "Go look in the closet." Hanging in the closet was a brand-new, full-length black and green wet suit that fit David perfectly.

When we went down to water ski, David asked if he could take the wet suit. I said, "No, it belongs to somebody else." But while we were waiting our turn to go out on the water, I said to

Jorie, "Why don't we let David wear the wet suit. It does seem pretty obvious that God provided it." So I told David that he could go put it on. He came back all decked out in the wet suit and was thoroughly pumped up. He knew there was a God in heaven who had answered his prayer. A few minutes later, David skied for the first time in his life.

All through the week we asked the Young Life staff if they knew who owned the wet suit. Incredibly, no one did. As we shared our find with more and more of the staff, many felt that God had simply supplied the wet suit in answer to David's prayers.

Do you know what I think happened? I think God looked down from heaven and saw a little 12-year-old boy praying his heart out in full faith that God would provide, and God thought, *How can I not provide this boy with a wet suit?*

God is looking for people who pray with such faith.

THE DARE

As you pray today, I want you to examine your faith. Do you believe like the centurion and my son that God will answer your prayer? If not, pray until you come to the place where you really believe that what you are asking is in God's will, and that God will meet your needs.

What did you pray today, believing that God will provide? Write this below.

_____

_____

_____

_____

_____

Can you record some prayers God answered in response to your faith?

_____

_____

_____

_____

_____

26

Learn When You Can Pray with Faith

Have faith in God. . . . I [Jesus] tell you, whatever you ask for in
prayer, believe that you have received it, and it will be yours.
MARK 11:22-24

My wife, Jorie, was a widow when I married her. She had married her first husband when she was just a junior in college. A couple months after getting married, her husband was diagnosed with inoperable spinal reticulum-cell sarcoma. Instead of enjoying honeymoon living, the newlyweds encountered a barrage of medical tests, surgeries, chemotherapy and pain medications.

In spite of the fact that he was not expected to win his battle with this dreadful cancer, they prayed for God to heal him and believed that God would. Godly professors from Wheaton College (which she attended) and Trinity University (which he attended) came and anointed him with oil and prayed for his healing. Thousands of people in the Chicago area and around the country lifted up prayers on his behalf. Every time people prayed for him, they grew in confidence that God was going to heal him. Even during his painful, final days, all of the pray-ers never lost their faith in God.

Nevertheless, after nearly two years of battling for his life, he died. Jorie told me that during his illness and after his death, one of the hardest things for her to handle was the guilt heaped on her by well-meaning but misguided Christians who said he could have been healed if she had just had enough faith. Enough faith? She had believed God would heal him right up to his last breath. What more could she have done?

This raises a question I hear frequently: "How come my prayer was not answered when I prayed in faith?" After all, Jesus said, "Have faith in God. . . . I tell you, whatever you ask for in prayer, believe that you have received it, and it will be yours" (Mark 11: 22-24). People who have prayed with faith but nevertheless have lost a loved one to cancer or some other dreaded disease wonder, *Was Jesus joking?* How do we reconcile Jesus' teaching with the reality of so many people who have prayed with faith for something and not seen their prayers answered? Of course Jesus was not joking, but how are we to understand His teaching that we will receive whatever we ask for in faith?

The importance of having faith and praying with faith was not something Jesus mentioned only once or twice. It permeated His teaching. For example, after Jesus exorcised a demon from a possessed boy who the disciples were unable to help, they asked Him why they had been unable to cast the demon out (I also mentioned this incident in chapter 8). Jesus answered, "Because you have so little faith. I tell you the truth, if you have faith as small as a mustard seed, you can say to this mountain, 'Move from here to there' and it will move. Nothing will be impossible for you" (Matt. 17:20-21).

Nothing? Then what happened to my wife's first husband? What gives here?

To understand Jesus' teaching about praying with faith, we need to read it in the light of other teachings in the Bible. Scripture also tells us that God does not promise to answer every prayer. If He were obliged to answer every petition, we would be sovereign, and He would be a servant doing our bidding. That wouldn't be right. We must remember the words of the teacher in Ecclesiastes: "God is in heaven and you are on earth" (Eccles. 5:2). God is God and we are not. God is not going to grant every petition we ask of Him.

Job cried for God to heal him and answer his questions. He received neither. Mary and Martha called for Jesus to come heal their brother. Instead, Jesus let Lazarus die, at least temporarily. The apostle Paul asked God to heal him, but God told him no. Paul wrote, "Three times I pleaded with the Lord to take it away from me. But he said to me 'My grace is sufficient for you, for my power is made perfect in weakness'" (2 Cor. 12:8-9). The Lord said in effect, "No, Paul. Even though you've healed many other people, I'm not going to grant you healing. I'm going to leave you with your disability and use you in spite of your illness. Just rely on my grace."

To further understand Jesus' teaching about praying with faith, we must pair it with John's teaching about it that we looked at in chapter 24: "If we ask anything according to his will, he hears us. And if we know that he hears us—whatever we ask—we know that we have what we asked of him" (1 John 5:14-15).

What do Jesus' and John's words together mean? Does God answer prayers of faith? Yes, but we cannot always pray with faith. When can we pray with faith? When we know absolutely that what we are requesting is in God's will. The only way my wife could pray with complete faith for God to heal her first husband was if she knew for certain it was God's will to heal him.

We can always pray with faith that God is willing and able to heal, but it is wise to add as Jesus did in the Garden of Gethsemane, "If it be your will" (see Matt. 26:39,42; Mark 14:36;

Luke 22:42). That's our way of admitting that we don't always know what's best. We can pray with faith for the salvation of someone, for we know it is God's will for everyone to come to salvation; but we have to add, "When and if it's your will," for we also know that God will not take away a person's freedom.

So remember, your ability to pray with faith is directly related to how closely you pray for things that are in God's will.

THE DARE

Today, I want you to begin to get in the practice of always making sure that what you are praying for is definitely in God's will. If you are struggling to really believe God will answer your prayers, maybe it's because you're not sure that what you are asking is in God's will. Because this is so important, once again I want you to write down requests you are praying for with faith and, next to it, why you believe your request is in God's will.

_____

_____

_____

_____

What things are in God's will that you can always pray for with faith? Make a list of these below.

_____

_____

_____

_____

_____

27

Praying When God Doesn't Seem to Answer

After Jesus had gone indoors, his disciples asked him privately,
"Why couldn't we drive it out?"

MARK 9:28

Why aren't some of our prayers answered? That's a question I am asked possibly more than any other. Soon after being asked, I find myself listening to stories from someone who is frustrated and perplexed by unanswered prayer. "I've pleaded with God for a baby, but I'm still childless." "I've asked God for a job for months, but I'm still unemployed." "I've cried out to God for my parents to get back together, but they're still getting a divorce." "I've prayed for my husband to stop drinking, but he still won't admit he's got a problem."

Nothing is more devitalizing than unanswered prayer. We call heaven, and no one seems to answer the phone.

We feel as forsaken as C. S. Lewis did when he grieved the loss of his wife to cancer:

> Meanwhile, where is God? This is one of the most disquieting symptoms. When you are happy, so happy that you have no sense of needing Him, . . . if you remember yourself and turn to Him with gratitude

and praise, you will be—or so it feels—welcomed with open arms. But go to Him when your need is desperate, when all other help is vain, and what do you find? A door slammed in your face, and a sound of bolting and double bolting on the inside. After that, silence. You may as well turn away.[1]

Who hasn't known such a desolating experience of unanswered prayer? What makes it worse is when the pray-er thinks, *I did everything I was supposed to do: I praised God, confessed my sins, believed, prayed in faith, rebuked the spiritual forces of evil, claimed God's promises, asked for something I thought was in God's will. I even fasted!* So why did God remain silent?

I once sat with a family who wondered about unanswered prayer. I first got to know them when I helped their son find Christ during his senior year in high school when I was his Young Life leader. Ten years after graduating from high school, still single, this young man was driving home one night when a car coming the opposite direction swerved into his lane and struck his car head-on. He lay in a coma for months. When he regained consciousness, it was painfully obvious that his life and his family's would be permanently altered. He could not talk, needed help feeding himself, needed someone to help him get dressed and undressed each day, and had to learn to walk again. During the next 10 years, he underwent numerous major surgeries. His parents, who had looked forward to leisure and travel in their retirement years, instead resigned themselves to the round-the-clock care their son required.

Many times they asked God to heal their son. During his final years, as his condition steadily worsened, they prayed that he might not have to suffer pain. But he was neither healed nor shielded from pain. To the day of his death, though, his family never stopped faithfully caring for him and never questioned their faith in God. They did, however, quietly wonder why their prayers went unanswered.

Almost every deathbed stands as a monument to a petition that was not granted.

We have already touched on some reasons why our prayers may not be answered: One reason may be because what we are asking is not good for us—God will not grant a request if He knows it will not be good for us. Another reason may be that He has something better for us (see chapter 4). Sometimes a no is just as much a sign of His love for us as a yes is. Another reason may be because we have asked for something outside His will (see chapter 24).

God turned down a request from the apostle Paul for healing. Paul had what he called "a thorn in his flesh," some kind of illness or disability (2 Cor. 12:7). Paul wrote, "Three times I pleaded with the Lord to take it away from me. But he said to me 'My grace is sufficient for you, for my power is made perfect in weakness'" (2 Cor. 12:8-9). God meant, "No, Paul, I plan to receive more glory by not healing you."

Another reason God may not answer our prayers is due to our disobedience. Sometimes we are in no position to ask anything of God, because we have not been obeying what He has asked of us (for a fuller discussion of this, see chapter 19).

Still another reason our prayers may not be answered is due to our lack of faith. Remember that faith is a prerequisite to answered prayer (see chapter 25).

Still another reason our prayers may go unanswered may be because our timing is wrong. God may be happy to grant what we request—but not yet. It is not His timing. He tells us to wait or slow down. By granting the petition at a later time, He will likely receive more glory or honor.

Sometimes God knows we are not yet prepared for what we have asked, and He knows that if He granted our petition, we couldn't handle what it would do to us. In such cases, it is God's grace and mercy that prevent our prayers from being answered. God withholds His gifts from us for our own good. Or perhaps God chooses to wait to purify our motives. Perhaps He is seeking to strengthen our character and test our faith. Perhaps He has unfinished business remaining with the person for whom we are praying.

Be careful not to insist that you know better than God about when a request should be granted. His delays are not necessarily denials. He has reasons for His "not yet." When we fly into a tantrum when God does not meet our demand for instant gratification, God simply shakes His head at our immaturity and says, "Kick and scream if you must, but you can't have what you want yet. Trust me. I know what I'm doing. I have my reasons."

A little boy asked his father for some roller skates. His dad bought him some. They were practice skates. The boy could skate on them, but they did not go very fast. The boy said, "Could you buy me some ball-bearing roller skates?" His dad replied, "You are a little young, son. Maybe in a year or two." But the boy kept up his pestering. Eventually the father's love got the better of his judgment.

On his birthday, when the boy opened his gifts, he was ecstatic when he found a box of ball-bearing roller skates. After that, all the other gifts meant nothing. He grabbed the skates and tried them out. He loved them. His father went out with him and warned him, "Son, I want you to know that these skates go much faster than the skates you had before. You must be very careful. If not, you'll end up in the street, and that could be very dangerous."

One day as the boy was skating, he was going too fast to make a turn, and he went flying out into the street. At that same moment, a sand truck came barreling down the road and mowed down the little boy. His father ran out to the street, picked up his little boy's limp body and carried him back into the house. As he sat holding his lifeless son, he prayed, "Father, next time I ask You for something and You say no, remind me that I may be asking for ball-bearing roller skates. You know when it is not the right timing."

The next time it appears as if God is not listening to your prayers, remember that He's listening, but He has His reasons for not necessarily answering when you want.

THE DARE

For today's challenge, I would like you to think about past prayers that went unanswered and the reasons why they may not have been answered. Write the unanswered requests down, and then note next to them some reasons why they may not have been answered. Could it be the request was not good, there was disobedience in your life, you lacked faith, or it was not the right timing?

What are some of your current requests that have not been answered? Write these down, and then next to each one, make notes of possible reasons why these requests have not been granted.

_____

_____

_____

_____

Note

1. C. S. Lewis, *A Grief Observed* (New York: Bantam Books, 1961), p. 4.

Pray Intelligently

When Hezekiah saw that Sennacherib had come and that
he intended to make war on Jerusalem, he consulted with his
officials and military staff about blocking off the water from
the springs outside the city, and they helped him.
2 CHRONICLES 32:2-3

Earlier in this book, we discussed Hezekiah's prayer said in reaction to threats from the king of Assyria (see chapter 20). But
Hezekiah did more than pray. He took steps to be part of the
answer to his prayer:

> When Hezekiah saw that Sennacherib had come and
> that he intended to make war on Jerusalem, he con-
> sulted with his officials and military staff about block-
> ing off the water from the springs outside the city, and
> they helped him. A large force of men assembled, and
> they blocked all the springs and the stream that flowed
> through the land. "Why should the kings of Assyria
> come and find plenty of water?" they said. Then he
> worked hard repairing all the broken sections of the wall
> and building towers on it. He built another wall outside
> that one and reinforced the supporting terraces of the
> City of David. He also made large numbers of weapons

and shields. He appointed military officers over the people and assembled them before him in the square at the city gate and encouraged them (2 Chron. 32:2-6).

Hezekiah cut off the water supply outside the city, fortified the city walls, increased his supply of weapons, and prepared the troops. He took steps to make conquering Jerusalem more difficult for the king of Assyria.

When Nehemiah learned that Jerusalem lay in rubble and the walls of the city were torn down, he wept and prayed for days (see chapter 22). But he too didn't just pray and expect God to do the rest. Between his prayer and the moment when he had an audience before the king, he went to work. He planned how long it would take him to rebuild the walls. He anticipated the opposition he would face in Judah, so he determined the official papers that would be required to grant him authority to rebuild the walls of Jerusalem. He estimated the supplies he would need to complete the wall. He figured out the number of horses that would be necessary to transport his men and supplies, and the number of soldiers he would need to protect them during their travel to Jerusalem. So when the king asked him how much it would cost and how long it would take, he had an answer ready (see Neh. 2:5-8).

Many people in the Bible practiced this principle of praying intelligently. Noah prayed, and then he built the ark. Joseph prayed for God to get him out of prison, and then he lived an exemplary life, so that the prison warden noticed him. Moses prayed, and then he went before Pharaoh and demanded that he let God's people go. David prayed, and then he charged out to fight Goliath. Solomon prayed, and then he built the Temple. Jehoshaphat prayed, and then he led his army out into battle. Peter and John and the New Testament church prayed, and then they went out and preached boldly.

Some people think that if they pray about something, God will take care of it, and they don't have to do anything else. That's not praying intelligently. Intelligent praying involves not only making our requests of God but also determining what we can do to help bring about an answer to our prayers.

Six of our nine children have played competitive tennis. Our oldest son, Tad, was a top-rated junior player and went to college on a tennis scholarship. Jorie took Tad to a tennis tournament when he was 11. Before taking the court, she gave him a little pep talk, as good tennis parents usually do. She told him to pray to Jesus during the match, and Jesus would help him. Tad proceeded to play probably the worst match in his life. He just stood there and got spanked by his opponent. After the match, Jorie asked him, "What was that? What happened out there?"

Tad said, "I prayed for Jesus to help me win the match, but He didn't answer my prayer." Jorie explained to him that putting our faith in Christ does not mean that we don't have to do anything. Christ would have been happy to help Tad, but Tad had to move his feet and swing his racquet.

Praying intelligently requires recognition that when we put our faith in Christ and pray for something, we must be part of the answer. We're not to simply walk away and expect God to do everything. God answers the prayer of the person who thinks and plans. He comes to the aid of the person who is willing to be part of the answer to prayer. God usually chooses to work with us and through us, not for us and without us. Prayer is never the substitute for human effort. We have to do our part. Prayer does not reduce the need for planning, preparation and hard work. We have to pray *and* act.

THE DARE

Today as you pray, I want you to think about what you can do to be part of the answer to your prayers. First, write down the concerns you have laid before God, and then next to it write what you can do to help with that particular problem.

Now I want you to do some planning. What are some steps you can take this week to help achieve the answers to your prayers? Jot down some of the steps you are going to take right now.

29

Pray with Passion

Oh, what a great sin these people have committed!
They have made themselves gods of gold. But now, please forgive their
sin—but if not, then blot me out of the book you have written.
EXODUS 32:31-32

According to Exodus 32, while Moses was up on Mount Sinai receiving the Ten Commandments, the people became restless and
said, "We don't know what's happened to Moses. Maybe he's dead!
Aaron, we don't like having a god we cannot see. Make us gods like
we saw in Egypt" (see Exod. 32:1). So Aaron asked the people to
bring him gold jewelry, which he cast into an idol in the shape of a
calf, and the people gathered around to worship the idol and in-
dulged in a drunken orgy. (Bad morals always follow bad theology.)

Meanwhile, up on the mountain, God told Moses that the
people had corrupted themselves:

> "I have seen these people," the LORD said to Moses, "and
> they are a stiff-necked people. Now leave me alone so that
> my anger may burn against them and that I may destroy
> them. Then I will make you into a great nation" (Exod.
> 32:9-10).

God was so angry that He wanted to destroy the people and make
Moses a new nation.

At God's command, Moses went down the mountain to see what the people had done. "When Moses approached the camp and saw the calf and the dancing, his anger burned and he threw the tablets out of his hands, breaking them to pieces at the foot of the mountain" (Exod. 32:19). Moses shattered on the ground the most priceless documents ever held by human hands. "And he took the calf they had made and burned it in the fire; then he ground it to powder, scattered it on the water and made the Israelites drink it" (Exod. 32:20). Moses made the people drink the bitter water so that they would never forget their faithlessness.

You may wonder what Aaron was thinking when he capitulated to the people's request to make an idol. So did Moses. He said to Aaron:

> "What did these people do to you, that you led them into such great sin?"
>
> "Do not be angry, my lord," Aaron answered. "You know how prone these people are to evil. They said to me, 'Make us gods who will go before us. As for this fellow Moses who brought us up out of Egypt, we don't know what has happened to him.' So I told them, 'Whoever has any gold jewelry, take it off.' Then they gave me the gold, and I threw it into the fire, and out came this calf'" (Exod. 32:21-24).

Aaron's excuse has to be one of the lamest excuses ever to fall from the lips of humankind.

After the people of Israel sinned by casting the golden idol and God wanted to destroy the people, Moses pleaded with God not to do that: "Oh, what a great sin these people have

committed! They have made themselves gods of gold. But now, please forgive their sin—but if not, then blot me out of the book you have written" (Exod. 32:31-32).

Can you believe it? Moses felt so strongly about God forgiving the people of Israel that he told God if God wasn't going to forgive them, then he, Moses, wanted God to take his name out of the book of life. That's praying like you mean it.

Have you ever felt so strongly about something that you prayed like that? Compared to Moses, our prayers seem bland and anemic. They fall flat. Could it be that we lack power in prayer because we do not feel strongly enough to really pray with passion?

A few years after I came to Sunset Presbyterian Church, the church had grown enough that I needed another pastor to work with me. So we formed a pastoral search team. We received hundreds of résumés from people all around the country, interviewed scores of them and invited several of them into town for a visit; but none of them seemed quite right for us. One night after we had been searching for nearly 18 months, I was really discouraged, so I cried out to God, "Lord, why is it taking so long? Surely there must be someone who can share the load. Our church can't keep growing if we don't find another pastor to help us. God, we need someone who loves Jesus, believes in the Scriptures, has a passion for reaching people who do not know Christ, loves people, is willing to put down roots in long-term ministry with us, and would love me and enjoy working with me." I prayed until I was confident that God had such a person. Once I was convinced that God had heard my prayer, my worries vanished. I felt certain that God was going to bring us just the right person. Within a week of that prayer, God brought to our attention the name of a Presbyterian pastor who was available. We interviewed and hired him, and he has been working with us for the last 22 years. He has been all the things I prayed for and more.

So how can you regularly pray as if you mean it? Let me share with you three practices that have helped me.

One, *pray out loud.* I am far more likely to pray with passion when I pray out loud. When I pray silently, I tend to daydream; but when I pray out loud, I stay focused on what I am saying to God. When I am alone with God, praying out loud has helped me pray with far more fervency and emotion.

Two, *pray with your body.* As human beings, we are composed of body, mind and spirit. When Christ calls us, He doesn't just want our spirits. He calls us to love Him with all our heart, soul, mind and strength. Far too often, though, we pray with just our minds. God calls us to pray to Him with our bodies as well.

The Bible is filled with examples of praying with the body. Moses fell prostrate before the Lord for 40 days and 40 nights, interceding for the people of Israel who had fashioned a golden idol (see Deut. 9:18-19). Moses prayed with his arms raised high as the Israelites battled the Amalekites (see Exod. 17:8-13). David danced before the Lord as the Ark was carried into Jerusalem (see 2 Sam. 6:12-16). Elisha prayed life back into the Shunammite boy by lying on top of him (see 2 Kings 4:32-35). The people who rebuilt the walls of Jerusalem with Nehemiah stood for hours in prayer as they rededicated themselves to the Lord (see Neh. 9). Jesus laid hands on many sick people when He prayed for them to be healed.

The most frequent prayer posture in the Bible is complete prostration with hands outstretched. The second most common posture is standing with the hands held high and the palms facing up. The third is kneeling before the Lord. These prayer postures alert us to the fact that body language is important if we hope to pray passionately.

C. S. Lewis suggests in *The Screwtape Letters* that one of Satan's schemes is to get us to believe that we can pray in whatever position we choose, for it makes no difference to the effectiveness of our prayers. That's simply not true. When I pray while I am lying down, my mind wanders or, worse yet, I fall asleep. When I pray with my eyes closed while sitting in a comfortable chair, the same thing happens. That hardly qualifies as passionate praying. I have discovered that kneeling is the position that best helps me to pray with passion. Kneeling is a symbol of humility before God and helps me remember how needy I am of God.

Third, *pray with concentration.* When I pray, I have to work hard to keep my mind from wandering. Thoughts dart in and out of my mind and easily distract me. I find that I have to get alone in a place where I will not be interrupted and all I have to think about is what I'm doing: praying.

I also find that I focus on my prayers better if I keep a pen and pad of paper handy. Instead of allowing random thoughts to distract me—especially of things I need to do—I simply jot the thoughts down on the pad of paper. Then I continue my prayers without fear of forgetting the to-dos.

THE DARE

Today I want you to engage in some practices that will help you pray like you mean it. Get alone in a place where you will not be heard or interrupted. Try praying out loud. Put your body into your prayer. Maybe try kneeling. Use some type of pillow or padding so that your knees do not hurt. Or try standing with your hands lifted to God. Or try walking around as you pray. The most extreme position would be to lie face down on the floor, prostrate before God. Keep a pad of paper and pen handy so that you can jot down thoughts you want to remember and then get right back to your prayers.

What steps are you going to use to help you pray like you mean it? Write these below.

_____

_____

_____

_____

_____

Try putting some emotion in your prayers to signal to God that you're really serious. Raise your voice or shed some tears—anything to show God that you're really serious about what you are praying. What did you choose to do? Write down what you did to put some passion in your prayers and what it felt like to do so.

_____

_____

_____

_____

_____

30

Pray with Desperation

"O our God, will you not judge them? For we have no power to face this vast army that is attacking us. We do not know what to do, but our eyes are upon you." All the men of Judah, with their wives and children and little ones, stood there before the LORD.

2 CHRONICLES 20:12-13

I received a letter from a couple who told me that things were so bad in their relationship with their son that their son would just hang up when they called. They finally quit trying and hadn't talked to him for eight years! Then this couple started attending our church and got involved in a care group where they learned how to pray, something that had been lacking in their lives. They started praying for their son, and the members of their small group prayed with them. One day after they had been praying for several months, they received a phone call from their son. He was in town and asked if he and his wife could stop by and go out to dinner with them. Within a year from that date, their relationship with their son and his wife improved so dramatically that they went on a weeklong vacation to New York together. Imagine that, after years of not talking to him! They had been desperate, so they cried out to God in prayer; and through prayer, they were able to reach a son they could not reach in any other way.

Jehoshaphat, the king of Judah, had faced a similar desperate situation when armies that far outnumbered the forces of Judah threatened the nation. What did Jehoshaphat do? He gathered the entire population to fast and pray:

> "O our God, will you not judge them? For we have no power to face this vast army that is attacking us. We do not know what to do, but our eyes are upon you." All the men of Judah, with their wives and children and little ones, stood there before the Lord (2 Chron. 20:12-13).

What a picture! Jehoshaphat, the people and their children didn't know what to do, so they stood there with their eyes upon God. (For a discussion of how important praise was in Jehoshaphat's prayer, see chapters 12 and 13.)

Maybe another reason we may lack power in our prayers (aside from not being passionate, as discussed in the last chapter) is because we are not desperate enough. Our situation may be desperate, but we're not.

Catherine grew up in a home where her family only went to church on holidays and where cultivating a personal relationship with Christ was a low priority. By the world's standards, she had everything she could wish for, including a beautiful house, fine clothes and a nice car. But she began to realize that something was missing in her life. She also noticed something remarkable about her maid, Ruby. Ruby always radiated peace and joy. She even sang hymns while she washed the kitchen floors. The more Catherine observed her behavior, the more intrigued she became. Eventually, she asked Ruby to tell her the secret of her contentment, and when she learned the answer, Catherine decided to follow Jesus, too.

Then Catherine began to have trouble with her teenaged daughter. The police arrested the daughter for breaking into a neighbor's home and stealing jewelry, and they found cocaine in

her purse. Catherine came back from the county jail, devastated. "Ruby, what am I going to do?" she sobbed. "How can I help her? It may be too late!"

Ruby said, "Child, Jesus already died for your daughter. There's no need for you to die, too."

"But, Ruby," Catherine protested, "you don't understand. I have prayed for her and nothing has happened."

"And how long have you been praying for your child?" Ruby asked.

"For at least six months, ever since I came to faith."

"And how long have I been working for you?"

"Ten years."

"That's right! And for nine years and six months, I have been on my knees washing these floors and praying for the salvation of this home! Don't you rush Jesus, girl! You give Him room, be patient and pray!"

"Well, I try to pray, and I use my prayer book, but I don't feel like anything happens," Catherine answered.

"You call that piddly stuff I hear you do praying?" Ruby asked.

"But, Ruby, you don't understand. I am desperate."

"Now we're talking prayer," Ruby responded.

Ruby knew that you don't really pray with power until you're desperate.

Some of the greatest prayers of the Bible were spoken by people who were desperate. Moses was desperate when he interceded for the sinful Israelites who were dancing before the golden calf (see Exod. 32). When Sennacherib threatened to destroy Jerusalem, King Hezekiah "tore his clothes and put on sackcloth" and cried out, "This day is a day of distress and rebuke and disgrace, as when children come to the point of birth and there is no strength to deliver them" (2 Kings 19:1,3). He was desperate (see 2 Kings

19; 2 Chron. 32). When the man went to his friend at midnight to ask for bread, he was desperate (see Jesus' teaching on prayer in Luke 11). Only when we're desperate are we likely to admit that we don't know what to do, so we cry out to God in prayer.

Once a week I meet with pastoral staff members who make up our church's management team. One week we each shared something we had written in our journals from our Bible reading for the week, and one of our youth pastors told us that he had written down 14 impossible situations that he had prayed about. Since he had just bared his soul by telling us about 14 impossible situations in his life, I suggested that we focus our prayers that morning on each of our own impossible situations. We prayed about problems in our marriages, struggles with our kids, difficult situations in the church, people who were very sick, and any other things that looked to us like impossible situations. Hearing the members of our management team cry out to God in desperation brought all of us to tears. But we all grew in confidence, because we realized our impossible situations were not impossible to God. God is waiting for us to cry to Him in desperation. Nothing is impossible for God.

THE DARE

Today I would like you to make a list of the impossible situations in your life in which you don't see any way for them to get resolved. Write down your impossible situations.

_____

_____

_____

_____

Now pray about them, verbalizing those impossible situations to God even though you don't know what to do. Wait upon God. How does verbalizing your impossible situations to God give you increased hope, because you realize nothing is impossible for God?

_____

_____

_____

_____

_____

31

Praying When Trust Is Gone

My heart is in anguish within me; the terrors of death assail me.
Fear and trembling have beset me; horror has overwhelmed me. If an
enemy were insulting me, I could endure it; if a foe were raising himself
against me, I could hide from him. But it is you, a man like myself,
my companion, my close friend, with whom I once enjoyed sweet
fellowship as we walked with the throng at the house of God.
PSALM 55:4-5,12-14

After the terrorist attack on New York City and Washington, DC, on September 11, 2001, the United States military launched an attack on Afghanistan to root out the Al-Qaida forces that were hiding there. One of the greatest fears our military had during the campaign was not the firepower of our enemies but friendly fire, misdirected American artillery.

Christians fear friendly fire as well. When we receive fire from our fellow soldiers, discouragement can set in quickly. When people we count as friends and supporters turn against us, we may become demoralized.

Friendly fire is exactly what happened to King David. When he reigned over Israel, his son Absalom stormed Jerusalem to seize power, and David fled the city with a few of his followers. David had known he had problems with his son Absalom. But what dismayed him even more than his son's mutiny was that several of his most trusted cabinet members betrayed him and switched loyalty to Absalom. Living in exile outside the city, David penned Psalm 55, a psalm of lament that reveals that David was in the pit of despair. He said that he could endure enemies attacking him, but attacks from his own son and several of his most trusted palace counselors he didn't know how to handle.

Nothing hurts more than when friends or family members turn on us. When that happens, we wonder if there is anyone we can trust. Psalm 55, however, tells us exactly who we can trust when all trust seems to be gone.

The first thing we learn from David's psalm is to *pour out our feelings to God.* David cried out to God:

> Hear me and answer me. My thoughts trouble me and I am distraught at the voice of the enemy, at the stares of the wicked; for they bring down suffering upon me and revile me in their anger. My heart is in anguish within me; the terrors of death assail me. Fear and trembling have beset me; horror has overwhelmed me (Ps. 55:2-5).

David didn't pull any punches. You can feel his pain. He was feeling afraid and lonely.

David told God that the worst thing about the whole ordeal was that he felt ambushed by his friends:

> If an enemy were insulting me, I could endure it; if a foe were raising himself against me, I could hide from him. But it is you, a man like myself, my companion, my close friend, with whom I once enjoyed sweet fellowship as we walked with the throng at the house of God (Ps. 55:12-14).

Those he had counted as reliable comrades had stabbed him in the back, and he denounced them: "But you, O God, will bring down the wicked into the pit of corruption; bloodthirsty and deceitful men will not live out half their days" (Ps. 55:23).

David's denunciation of his enemies may seem a bit drastic, but it actually marks an advance in his spiritual growth, because he consciously brought God into his experience. We take a step forward spiritually anytime we pour out our troubled thoughts to God.

The second thing we learn from David is to *put our trust in God.* David fled from his palace in fear for his life. He was sick over the fact that some of his friends, along with his son, had betrayed him. But in the midst of his despair, he resolved to trust God:

> But I call to God, and the LORD saves me. Evening, morning and noon I cry out in distress, and he hears my voice. He ransoms me unharmed from the battle waged against me, even though many oppose me (Ps. 55:16-17).

David had a hard time making sense of why God had allowed David's own son and some of his best staff to turn against him; but instead of running from God in anger, he drew near to God, determined to trust God:

> Cast your cares on the LORD and he will sustain you; he will never let the righteous fall. . . . But as for me, I trust in you (Ps. 55:22-23).

The last line of the psalm, "But as for me, I trust in you," is the greatest line in the psalm, and it is true prayer. Even though God had not yet answered David's prayer and David was surrounded by enemies, he knew that God's miracle of deliverance would come. By meditating on God, David came to the place of faith.

THE DARE

Are there some things that are troubling you? Are there things that are not going well? Today I want you to pour out your feelings to God. Tell Him everything you are feeling. Don't hold anything back, thinking that it is not very Christian to be blunt about our feelings. After you have prayed, write down some of the things you told God today.

_____

_____

_____

_____

_____

Why do you think it might benefit your relationship with God to be honest in expressing your feelings to Him like David, rather than stuffing them? Write down some reasons below.

_____

_____

_____

_____

_____

32

Be Transparent

*Be merciful to me, LORD, for I am faint; O LORD, heal me, for my bones
are in agony. My soul is in anguish. I am worn out from groaning;
all night long I flood my bed with weeping and drench my couch with
tears. My eyes grow weak with sorrow; they fail because of all my foes.*
PSALM 6:2-3,6-7

Psalm 6 is another one of David's psalms of lament, and as in so
many of his psalms, David here told God exactly how he felt: "Be
merciful to me, LORD, for I am faint; O LORD, heal me, for my
bones are in agony. My soul is in anguish. I am worn out from
groaning; all night long I flood my bed with weeping and drench
my couch with tears. My eyes grow weak with sorrow; they fail
because of all my foes" (Ps. 6:2-3,6-7). He was a mess. Fortunately,
he knew that he could trust God; but in the meantime, he was
honest and blunt and let all of his complaints out. This is typical
of a psalm of lament, which usually has five elements:

1. A cry for help
2. The lament, in which we learn about the problem the
   psalmist is facing
3. A petition, in which the psalmist makes his request
   of God
4. A confession of trust, in which the psalmist tells God
   that he trusts Him in spite of the situation he is facing

5. A vow of praise, in which the psalmist vows to praise
   God in the midst of his crisis

Notice the progression. It begins with a crisis that causes a call
to God for help, and it ends with praise that shows confidence
that God will answer the psalmist's petition.

An important prerequisite to confidence and praise, however, is the lament. David was very transparent with God in
pouring out his feelings. He told God exactly what he was feeling and thinking. He was honest with God.

Although we don't know exactly when David wrote this
psalm, we do know that David was very sad when he wrote
these words. We do know that David was totally transparent
before God in his prayer. And we do know that the fact that
this psalm and many others like it are in Scripture (about 40
percent of the psalms are laments) means that God invites us
to be transparent with Him. He wants us to be honest with
Him when we pray.

It's always refreshing when people are transparent with us,
isn't it? One of the things I love about my wife is how honest
she is about her feelings. She began her first book, *The Power of
Modeling*, with just such transparency:

> As a pastor's wife and the mother of four young boys, I
> find that early mornings are the most action-packed
> hours of my days. Our two oldest hate to be late for
> school, often putting pressure on all of us. One morn-
> ing it looked as though our carpool driver had forgot-
> ten us. "If Geoff doesn't come in five minutes, I'll take
> you," I agreed. Our second and fourth graders, jackets
> zipped and backpacks in position, stood glued to our

window, anxiously scanning the streets for our neighbor's car.

It's 8:04, I noticed, as I turned to gather shoes and socks for barefooted Luke and to fold a diaper for Joel in case I needed to drive. I quickly dressed and brushed my hair.

Only makeup to go, and I'll grab my purse and keys and . . . The phone interrupted my mental countdown. I answered it, amid protest from 10-year-old Tad. "Don't, Mom! If you talk, we'll be late for sure."

The caller was the acquisitions editor from NavPress. I had been praying for an opportunity to talk to her about my manuscript on parenting. I glanced at the clock, groaning inwardly. If I took the call, my boys would certainly be late for school. On the other hand, I didn't want to miss the opportunity this phone call might provide. I ran to retrieve my manuscript and then to retreat to my bedroom, hurriedly explaining to eight-year-old David to hang up the kitchen phone. Further sensing a need for quiet, I plopped Joel in his downstairs playpen and instructed four-year-old Luke to keep him happy. I bolted past Tad on the stairway, an apologetic look lining my face. His look registered desperation, nearing tears.

A fleeting thought reminded me of my prayer for a peaceful conversation with this editor. I had rehearsed the conversation several times in my mind, never anticipating these circumstances. Already I could see I was in for trouble.

I wanted to speak clearly. Instead I gasped little breaths after nervously chasing up the stairs twice looking for my manuscript. Either David didn't hear me ask him to hang up the phone, or worse, he forgot, because the kitchen phone remained off the hook throughout our conversation. In the middle of our discussion, Tad and David began arguing, oblivious to the phone lying open on the counter next to them. All composure gone, they hollered, kicking and wrestling on the floor. Sensing the tension, Joel began screaming from his playpen. Luke seized his moment and skipped from room to room, singing loudly, his voice increasing and fading as he rounded his laps.

All these sounds projected through the phone, clearly heard by the editor whom I hoped would publish my book on parenting! Not only did I fail to speak well, I could barely think. I felt my opportunity was ruined.

I drove my boys to school in silence, fifteen minutes after the bell rang. I was too upset to pray with them, and barely mumbled, "Bye." What a disaster! I felt humiliated. Tears stung my hot cheeks as I pondered what right I had to write a book for parents when events like these happened in my own family. I was painfully aware that I am far from a perfect parent.[1]

This sort of transparency has attracted many readers to Jorie's book, and this sort of transparency is what attracts God's attention. Transparency with God in prayer means being honest with God, sharing with God how you feel about things.

THE DARE

Being honest with God is such a big part of growing with God in prayer. So today, I want you to be totally honest and transparent about what you're dealing with in your life right now and how you feel about your situation.

How are you feeling about your work?

_____

_____

_____

_____

_____

What are you worried about with your family?

_____

_____

_____

_____

_____

What concerns do you have about your health?

_____

_____

_____

_____

_____

What makes you anxious about your finances?

_____

_____

_____

_____

_____

David didn't hold back in sharing his feelings, and you shouldn't either. After you have answered these questions and prayed about them, write down some of the feelings you shared with God during that time.

_____

_____

_____

_____

_____

_____

Note

1. Jorie Kincaid, *The Power of Modeling* (Colorado Springs, CO: *NavPress,* 1989), pp. 13-14.

33

Praying When You Are Afraid

I am in the midst of lions; I lie among ravenous beasts—men whose
teeth are spears and arrows, whose tongues are sharp swords. . . .
They spread a net for my feet—I was bowed down in distress.
PSALM 57:4-6

David wrote Psalm 57 when he feared for his life. Years before, he had killed the giant Goliath and had become very popular with the people of Israel. "Saul has killed thousands; David has killed ten thousands," the people sang (see 1 Sam. 18:7). The fact that people loved David more than Saul enraged Saul, and he burned with jealousy toward David. So he sought to kill him. Fearing for his life, David fled into the mountains and hid in a cave.

All kinds of things can cause us to be afraid. We might fear an ominous medical diagnosis. We might be afraid of dying. We might fear being rejected by a date, a mate or one of our children. We might fear being laid off or fired from a job. We might even fear approaching God, but in Psalm 57, David gives us three helpful suggestions for how to pray when we are afraid. All we have to remember are three words.

The first word is "lament." Psalm 57 is another psalm of lament, similar to the psalms we discussed in chapters 31 and 32. In the psalm, David told God that he was afraid:

Have mercy on me, O God, have mercy on me. I am in the midst of lions; I lie among ravenous beasts—men whose teeth are spears and arrows, whose tongues are sharp swords. . . . They spread a net for my feet—I was bowed down in distress (Ps. 57:1,4-6).

Try to feel what David felt. King Saul and his army had been chasing David all through the countryside. He felt as if he were in the midst of ferocious animals. Can you sense his terror? His danger was great, and the cry he delivered was urgent, for it was twice uttered. David was in deep distress, and he poured out his heart to God and cried to God for deliverance.

When you are afraid, tell God what you're feeling and pour out your heart to Him in prayer. Cry out to Him; *lament* your situation. The importance of this cannot be overemphasized, because if you are going to grow deeper with God in prayer, you have to learn to be open and honest with Him about your feelings.

The second word you have to remember is "trust." David wrote:

I will take refuge in the shadow of your wings until the disaster has passed. I cry out to God Most High, to God, who fulfills his purpose for me. He sends from heaven and saves me, rebuking those who hotly pursue me; God sends his love and his faithfulness (Ps. 57:1-3).

What David meant was that he would take shelter in the shade of God's outstretched protection. David was confident that God would hear his cry and would save him from his enemy.

The amazing thing about this psalm is that in the midst of such trying circumstances, David was able to maintain a firm confidence in God. David was running for his life from Saul and hiding in a cave. He was scared of the enemies all around him; but rather than focusing on them, he fixed his mind on God and God's attributes of love and faithfulness. He made a choice. Rather than choosing to fret and worry, he chose to think about God's mercy and protection.

In the wake of the 9/11 terrorist attack on the United States, many Americans found courage to go on through the music of Bono, the lead singer of U2, who sang that year for a TV audience of 130 million at the Super Bowl half-time show and was the recipient of several Grammy awards. In "Peace on Earth," he mourned, "Sick of sorrow, I'm sick of the pain, I'm sick of hearing again and again that there's gonna be peace on Earth."[1] In "Walk On," he sang, "I know it aches and your heart it breaks and you can only take so much. Walk on."[2]

Your expression of trust in God in prayer indicates that even though there are things going on in your life that cause you to be afraid, you choose to put your confidence in God that He will take care of you. Rather than shriveling up in fear, you choose to walk on.

The third and most courageous word to remember is "praise." (The surprise in this psalm—and in all psalms of lament—is that practically all of them end in praise.) *Praise comes after we pour out our feelings to God—lamenting* our circumstances and committing to put our *trust* in Him. After David told God how afraid he was and how he would trust God no matter what, he praised God: "Be exalted, O God, above the heavens; let your glory be over all the earth" (Ps. 57:5). The word "exalt" comes from the Hebrew word *rum* and means "to be high or to make high." God is on high and He is made even higher by our praise. Praise elevates God.

Then David went even further in his praise: "My heart is steadfast, O God, my heart is steadfast; I will sing and make music. Awake, my soul! Awake, harp and lyre! I will awaken the dawn" (Ps. 57:7-8). Think for a moment and remember that David wrote this when he was hiding in the back of a cave. He could have had a pity party and felt sorry for himself, but instead he *chose* to praise God. He had to rouse himself, to will himself, to praise.

One other thing about praise in the psalms: It is not just some general expression of jubilation. Praise is always directed to God. And that's exactly what David did:

I will praise you, O Lord, among the nations; I will sing of you among the peoples. For great is your love, reaching to the heavens; your faithfulness reaches to the skies. Be exalted, O God, above the heavens; let your glory be over all the earth (Ps. 57:9-11).

David praised God for His greatness.

One summer during college I worked as a cook at a restaurant. I usually worked the swing shift, often until one or two in the morning. One night very late, a guy who was drunk and angry came in. Something one of the waitresses said ticked him off, and somehow he got into the cook station and grabbed a big cutting knife. Flashing the huge knife around, he stood at one end of the cook's station, and I stood at the other end. I was scared to death, but I remember praying, "God, save us."

The manager grabbed a pot of scalding coffee and threw it at the man, but that just further enraged him. Fortunately, someone had been able to call 9-1-1, and the police arrived and quickly took the man into custody, thankfully before anyone got seriously hurt.

I was still shaking as I drove home, but as I revisited the terrifying sequence of events in my mind, I began to praise God for protecting me and all the people in the restaurant. And as I began to praise God for His power and protection, I felt the muscles in my body begin to relax. My lament and trust led to praise—I (and the others) had been protected, and God had been exalted.

THE DARE

Today I would like you to reflect on the things that you fear. What things worry you and cause you to feel afraid? Tell God about them. Pour out your heart to Him. Make them your lament to God. Don't hold back. Be completely upfront with God. What are some of the fears you shared with Him?

_____

_____

_____

_____

Why is honestly sharing your fears and worries with God not a step back but a step forward in prayer?

_____

_____

_____

_____

Notes

1. Adam Clayton, David Evans (The Edge), Paul David Hewson (Bono) and Laurence Mullen, Jr., "Peace on Earth," © 2000 Universal Music Publishing International, Ltd., performed by U2 on the album *All That You Can't Leave Behind*.
2. Ibid.

34

Praying Against the Spiritual Forces of Evil

For our struggle is not against flesh and blood, but against the rulers,
against the authorities, against the powers of this dark world and
against the spiritual forces of evil in the heavenly realms.
EPHESIANS 6:12

Until we recognize that many of the problems we encounter with people in this world involve the spiritual forces of evil and that the only way to win the battle against those forces is through prayer, we will not spend the time in prayer that we should. The apostle Paul said, "For our struggle is not against flesh and blood, but against the rulers, against the authorities, against the powers of this dark world and against the spiritual forces of evil in the heavenly realms" (Eph. 6:12). Paul says the forces of darkness are real, cunning, powerful and wicked.

Make no mistake that Satan is trying to destroy humankind in any way he can. He attacks our marriages. He tries to get our sons and daughters to make choices that will ruin their lives. He tries to suck us into sin, so that we feel so guilty and so like hypocrites that we won't even whisper to people a word about Christ. In fact, Satan works tirelessly to keep people in this world from knowing Jesus: "The god of this age has blinded the minds of unbelievers, so that they cannot see the light of the gospel of the glory of Christ" (2 Cor. 4:4). In order to rescue people from darkness, we have to subdue the forces of evil.

Jim Cymbala shares a very dramatic example of a battle he and the members of his church, the Brooklyn Tabernacle in New York City, had with forces of evil:

One Tuesday night two members of the church brought a teenager to the prayer meeting who, they said, was on drugs and needed to be delivered. That's all they told me. I didn't think too much about it; this kind of thing happens often.

About a half hour into the meeting, after we had been worshiping for a while, I said, "There's a girl here who's been brought by some members, and they'd like her to be prayed for; she's hooked on drugs."

These members began walking toward the front with a short Hispanic girl. She seemed in a daze—the effect of drugs, I assumed. Her name was Diana.

I was standing, as I usually do on Tuesday nights, on the ground level with the people, at the head of the center aisle. All of a sudden, I began to tense up; alarm bells seemed to be going off in my spirit, signifying that something was wrong—something was about to happen.

I noticed off to my right a visiting evangelist I knew. I said to her, "Amy, it's good to see you here tonight. Would you come help me pray for the young lady?" As she moved out of her seat, the Holy Spirit came upon her, and she sensed the same anticipation. We were suddenly both on "red alert" for some unknown reason.

One of the associate pastors joined us, and we laid hands on Diana and began to pray. "O Jesus, help us," I said quietly.

Like a shot, the mention of Jesus' name brought an explosion of rage and screaming. The five-foot-one-inch girl lunged for my throat, throwing back the two friends who had guided her up the aisle. Before I knew what was happening, I had been body-slammed against the front edge of the platform. Diana ripped the collar right off my white shirt as if it were a piece of tissue. A hideous voice from deep inside her began to scream, "You'll never have her! She's ours! Get away from her!" The language then turned obscene.

Some in the congregation stood and began to pray aloud. Others gasped. Some covered their eyes. Meanwhile, several deacons jumped up and tried to pull her off of me. Despite her size, she fought all of us with tremendous strength.

We finally managed to subdue her. Amy, the evangelist, began to pray fervently. I leaned over the girl to address the spirits: "Shut up! In the name of Jesus, come out of her!" I demanded.

Diana's eyes rolled back in her head, and twice she spit directly into my face, no more than a foot away. The church kept earnestly calling out to God for his help. Clearly, we were not battling some imaginary "spirit of anger" or whatever. This was a classic case of demon possession.

Within a few minutes, the girl was set totally free. She stopped cursing; her body relaxed. We relaxed our grip on her, and she gently stood up to raise her hands and begin praising the Lord. Soon she was singing, with the rest of us, "Oh, the blood of Jesus! It washes white as snow," as tears streamed down her cheeks, ruining her makeup.

Diana has been serving the Lord for ten years now in the church.[1]

God delivered Diana from Satan in response to the prayers of faithful believers. Through prayer, we call forth the powers of God to defeat the forces of evil and see breakthrough.

THE DARE

Today as you pray, I want you to be aware that you are doing battle with the spiritual forces of evil. As you pray for people, ask God to push back the spiritual forces of evil, because Jesus won the decisive victory over them on the cross. When you pray for unbelievers, ask God to lift the blinders Satan has put over their eyes so they can see their need for Christ. When you pray for believers, ask God to protect them from the evil one who wants to devour them like a roaring lion. Make sure you take time to praise God for His great power, because praise sends the forces of darkness scurrying.

How did you pray against the forces of evil today?

_____

_____

_____

_____

What answers to prayer have you seen recently?

_____

_____

_____

_____

_____

Note

1. Jim Cymbala with Dean Merrill, *Fresh Wind, Fresh Fire: What Happens When God's Spirit Invades the Heart of His People* (Grand Rapids, MI: Zondervan, 1997), pp. 109-110.

35

Pray with Fasting

When you fast, put oil on your head and wash your face,
so that it will not be obvious to men that you are fasting,
but only to your Father, who is unseen; and your Father,
who sees what is done in secret, will reward you.
MATTHEW 6:17-18

Just a cursory reading of the Bible reveals that many of the most impassioned prayers in the Bible were accompanied by fasting. Moses fasted and prayed before the Lord for 40 days and 40 nights because of all the sins of the people of Israel (see Deut. 9:18). When Nehemiah heard that the walls of Jerusalem were torn down and the city lay in ruins, he mourned and fasted and prayed for days (see Neh. 1:4). Before Esther went to plead with King Xerxes for her people, she fasted for three days and three nights (see Esther 4:16). When Daniel cried out for God to restore the people of Israel to Jerusalem, He "pleaded with [God] in prayer and petition, in fasting, and in sackcloth and ashes" (Dan. 9:3). Another time he fasted and prayed for three weeks (see Dan. 10:2-3). Jesus did battle with the devil during a 40-day fast, and then Jesus "returned to Galilee in the power of the Spirit" (Luke 4:14). God responded mightily when these prayers were accompanied by fasting.

If fasting was an important practice for biblical characters, why do we hear so little about it today? Why do most Christians live as if the biblical texts that address fasting have been torn out of their

Bibles? I think it is partly because we assume that fasting is an Old Testament practice and is no longer relevant today. I also think it is partly due to our thinking that it's a vestige of false asceticism: We see that the practice of fasting in many Eastern religions is based on the assumption that the body is bad and pleasure is to be avoided, but we know that the body is good and that pleasure is a gift from God. Whatever the current reason for not fasting, Jesus assumed that His followers *would* fast:

> When you fast, put oil on your head and wash your face, so that it will not be obvious to men that you are fasting, but only to your Father, who is unseen; and your Father, who sees what is done in secret, will reward you (Matt. 6:17-18).

Notice that Jesus said "when," not "if."

Although the 12 disciples did not fast while Jesus was alive, Jesus did say that they too would fast—after He ascended into heaven:

> John's disciples came and asked [Jesus], "How is it that we and the Pharisees fast, but your disciples do not fast?"
>
> Jesus answered, "How can the guests of the bridegroom mourn while he is with them? The time will come when the bridegroom will be taken from them; then they will fast" (Matt. 9:14-15).

Jesus meant that the apostles, like guests of a bridegroom, didn't need to fast yet, because He (the Bridegroom) was still with them. Once Jesus was gone, fasting would be called for.

I think we would experience far more power in prayer if we returned to the practice of fasting. During the past 30 years, I have

made it my practice to go without food one day a week, to give myself to the study of God's Word, to memorize Scripture, to pray and, since I am a pastor, to message preparation. I always set a prayer goal as the reason for my fast. I have experienced amazing answers to prayer through this combination of prayer and fasting.

Fasting has also heightened my spiritual sensitivity. When I fast, I find that my mind is keener, so I am able to focus better and longer when I pray. Fasting has enabled me to be more aware of Christ's power over the spiritual forces of evil and has preceded some of my greatest spiritual victories. I have fasted before many important speaking engagements, and I believe that God blessed my speaking with the power of His Holy Spirit. I remember one time in particular when I fasted and prayed before speaking to a large group, and I asked God what He would have me speak about. I believe God directed me as to what I should say and spoke through me, as many people made commitments to Christ that night.

What is it about fasting that increases our power in prayer? Am I suggesting that we earn God's favor by starving ourselves to death? Am I suggesting that we have to impress God and beg God to give us what we need?

We don't have to earn God's favor, but fasting is a means of signaling to God and ourselves that we really mean business in our prayers. For me, fasting is a means of making more time to pray, since I don't have to take time for meal preparation and cleanup. If I have a serious problem I am facing, I declare a day of fasting and take the problem before the Lord.

When Jesus taught about fasting, He gave some instructions so that we wouldn't go awry in our practice. He warned us to keep our fasting secret and not to do it just so people would look at us and say, "My, that person is fasting so hard." He continues, "But when you fast, put oil on your head and wash your face, so that it will not be obvious to men that you are fasting, but only to your Father who is unseen; and your Father, who sees what is done in secret, will reward you" (Matt. 6:17-18).

In the first century, putting oil on the face was essential, as a person's skin would get very dry in the desert. One of the Essenic cults had a saying: "God loves rough faces." They didn't put oil on their faces, and they didn't wash either (they must have thought God likes smelly faces, too). They looked somber and haggard so people would know they were fasting. Jesus said not to do that. He told people to wash their faces and put oil on their heads so no one would know they were fasting.

The most important thing to remember about fasting is that God is interested in healthy fasting done in secret to draw us into a closer relationship with Him. God is not interested in anorexia or bulimia, and He's not interested in reviving cultic ways of fasting that show to the world what a person is doing. (A word of caution: Before going on a fast, consult your doctor to make sure that you are healthy enough to fast.)

Healthy fasting is done in secret before God alone. It's a discipline we engage in to get closer to God. It is something we do that gives us more time to study God's Word, pray to God and listen to God.

And the great thing is that aside from gaining a closer relationship with God, we'll gain special power in our prayers.

THE DARE

Today, I would like you to consider setting aside a day to fast and pray. What issues or problems are you facing in your life

where you say, "I don't know what to do?" It's one of those "only by prayer" situations we talked about in chapter 8. It's a problem so big and so important to you that you are willing to go without food for a day to give yourself more time to pray about it. It has to be a day when you will have some time to slow down and pray. Think about a day in the next couple of weeks that you could set aside to fast and pray.

What day did you choose? Write that date down below.

_____

_____

_____

_____

_____

What problems, issues or struggles are you facing that will be the focus for your day of fasting?

_____

_____

_____

_____

_____

Why and how would fasting improve your relationship with God?

_____

_____

_____

_____

_____

36

Pray for Our Leaders

I urge, then, first of all, that requests, prayers, intercession and thanksgiving be made for everyone—for kings and all those in authority, that we may live peaceful and quiet lives in all godliness and holiness.

1 TIMOTHY 2:1-2

As believers, we are not to be enemies of the state. Nor are we to worship our leaders. We do something far more important: We pray for our leaders.

Most Christians overlook this New Testament instruction. Instead, I usually find one of two attitudes. One is apathy. Many believers are apolitical, and they want to remain uninvolved and uninformed. The other attitude is cynicism. Cynical believers are critical of their national or local leaders but don't necessarily do anything to effect changes.

Paul suggested a better way to be: compliant and prayerful.

Everyone must submit himself to the governing authorities, for there is no authority except that which God has established. The authorities that exist have been established by God (Rom. 13:1).

I urge, then, first of all, that requests, prayers, intercession and thanksgiving be made for everyone—for kings and all those in authority (1 Tim. 2:1-2).

Since we recognize that those who govern us have been established by God, we are to pray for them. Whether we voted for them or support their political platform doesn't matter.

Carl Sandberg, in his five-volume work on the life of Abraham Lincoln, tells us that out of 54 pastors in Springfield, Illinois in 1860, not one voted for Abraham Lincoln. Nevertheless, out of obedience to God, they covenanted to get together to pray for their president, and he became possibly the greatest president our country has ever known.

Scripture suggests that the key to a great presidency may not be so much the views, leadership or capabilities of the president but the prayers of God's people. According to 2 Chronicles 7:14, "If my people, who are called by my name, will humble themselves and pray and seek my face and turn from their wicked ways, then will I hear from heaven and will forgive their sin and will heal their land." The health of our country, or any nation, lies not so much with the president and his (or her) cabinet but with the decisions and prayers of God's people. We like to blame what is happening in our country on our leaders. But we fail to recognize that our leaders are a reflection of us. We voted them into office. God is looking for Christ followers who are devoted to Him and give themselves to praying for their leaders.

In their hit song "What If His People Prayed?" the Christian band Casting Crowns suggest that praying would make a huge difference for our land:

What if His people prayed
And those who bear His name
Would humbly seek His face, yeah,
And turn from their own way?
He said that He would hear,

His promise has been made,
He'll answer loud and clear, yeah,
If only we would pray.

This sentiment is echoed by God: "I looked for a man among them who would build up the wall and stand before me in the gap on behalf of the land so I would not have to destroy it, but I found none" (Ezek. 22:30). God is looking for people who will stand in the gap by praying for their country and its leaders.

Maybe you're wondering how our prayers can make a difference in our country. Paul suggested three good things that happen when God's people pray.

One, our country will be more likely to achieve peace and security: "[so] that we may lead peaceful and quiet lives" (1 Tim. 2:2). By praying for our country and its leaders, our nation has a better chance of being granted peace and security by God. If our country is not filled with unrest, then we will be able to lead peaceful lives.

Two, Christians will be more likely to live "in all godliness and holiness" (1 Tim. 2:2). By praying for our leaders, we increase the likelihood of God granting us conditions where we can pursue reverence and devotion to goodness and righteousness.

Three, we increase the likelihood of more people finding salvation in Christ: "This is good, and pleases God our Savior, who wants all men to be saved and to come to a knowledge of the truth" (1 Tim. 2:3-4). God is pleased when a nation has peace and God's people live in godliness and holiness, for these are the best conditions for people to come to the knowledge of the truth about Christ. Throughout history, the gospel of Jesus Christ has spread most rapidly during times of peace. During times of turmoil or war, missionaries are often kicked out of countries, believers are forced underground and people are not allowed to pass freely across borders. When countries are at peace within their borders and with each other, the gospel is able to move more easily within a country and from one country to another. The 1850s in the United States are a good example of this.

The 1850s in the United States brought a marked decline in spirituality in America. The discovery of gold in California turned many people's minds away from spiritual matters to material matters. Political turmoil between the North and the South over the issue of slavery and other things threatened to destroy the unity of our nation. A severe financial panic led to even greater concern about material things.

Then in September 1857, a businessman named Jeremiah Lanphier decided to invite other businessmen to join him for a noonday prayer meeting once a week, seeking a renewing work of the Holy Spirit. He distributed hundreds of handbills advertising the meeting, but the first day only half a dozen people showed up at the meeting in the rear of a church on Fulton Street in New York City. About two weeks later, there were 40 participants, and within six months, some 10,000 were gathered daily for prayer in New York City alone. A spiritual awakening swept the country, and within two years an estimated one million people had professed faith in Christ. And it all began with prayer—for our country, our leaders and our people.

THE DARE

Today I want you to pray for your leaders (even if you don't agree with their politics or policies). Pray that God would help all of them do His will on earth. Pray for your president and

vice president. Pray for your congressmen and women. Pray for your state and local leaders. Pray for the members of the Supreme Court.

What are some of the names of your leaders? Write these below and then covenant with God to pray for them regularly.

_____

_____

_____

_____

_____

What concerns do you have about your city, state and country? Write them down and commit to praying about these things at least once a week.

_____

_____

_____

_____

_____

3 7

Pray for Justice

*He has showed you, O man, what is good.
And what does the* LORD *require of you? To act justly and
to love mercy and to walk humbly with your God.*
MICAH 6:8

In April 2004, Kenyan Member of Parliament Maoka Maore received a mysterious phone call telling him how he could discover some interesting paperwork that would expose a scandal in the Kibaki government. The first document was a copy of a 2002 tender, or bidding opportunity, opened up by the previous government to supply Kenya with a computerized passport printing and lamination system. Nothing strange there—in the wake of Al Qaeda's 1998 bombing of the US embassy in Nairobi, Washington had been pressing Kenya (seen as a soft target for Islamic extremists filtering in from Somalia) to upgrade its passport system and better monitor its borders. The highest bid for that tender had been made by De La Rue, a British company, while the lowest came from Face Technologies, an American firm. What was strange, if the second document Maore obtained was to be believed, was that the bid had gone to neither company. Instead a payment voucher showed a Central Bank down payment to a British company called Anglo Leasing and Finance Company Limited. This oddity was just a sign of things yet to be revealed.

The final contract, it turned out, was a bloated, murky thing and was worth $34 million, nearly three and a half times as much as the lowest bid (which the government would ordinarily be expected to accept). When he (and others) traveled to England to check out the company that had been awarded the contract, they found there was no business at the address in the contract. It turned out that there was no company at all. Maore said that it was like a dream in which you pull the tail of a snake, and you find that it just goes on and on forever. He ended up finding corruption in the highest reaches of government.[1] Government leaders—who the people were supposed to be able to trust—were just paying themselves, fattening their wallets on the backs of the people.

God notices when government leaders are corrupt, for His commands apply to all people. He doesn't have one set of rules for leaders and rulers and another set for common people. His statutes apply to all people: "He has showed you, O man, what is good. And what does the LORD require of you? To act justly and to love mercy and to walk humbly with your God" (Mic. 6:8).

When King David sinned by committing adultery with Bathsheba and by murdering her husband, Uriah, the prophet Nathan came to the palace to confront David. He told the king a story about a rich man who had a very large number of sheep and cattle and a poor man who had nothing except one little ewe lamb he had bought. He raised it, and it grew up with him and his children. It shared his food, drank from his cup and even slept in his arms. It was like a daughter to him. Now a traveler came to the rich man, but the rich man refrained from taking one of his own sheep or cattle to prepare a meal for the traveler who had come to him. Instead, he took the ewe lamb that belonged to the poor man and prepared it for the one who had come to him. David burned with anger against the man and said to Nathan, "As surely as the LORD lives, the man who did this deserves to die! He must pay for that lamb four times over, because he did such a thing and had no pity" (2 Sam. 12:5-6).

Nathan replied in one of the most famous lines in all the Bible: "You are the man!" (2 Sam. 12:7). He told David, "You're the one who did this. You stole Uriah's wife and killed Uriah. Your house will be marked by violence" (see 2 Sam. 12:9-10). Nathan delivered this condemnation to the king of Israel. In any other country in the world in that day, Nathan would have been beheaded. But not in Israel. In Israel, Nathan could say this to the king of Israel, because both the king and the people stood under the Law.

Even a cursory reading of the Bible reveals that God hates corruption and injustice, not only among leaders but also among all people. And leaders and common people alike are not only "to act justly," but we are also to pray for justice. Isaiah complained to the people of Judah and Israel, "No one calls for justice; no one pleads his case with integrity. They rely on empty arguments and speak lies; they conceive trouble and give birth to evil" (Isa. 59:4). Isaiah was disappointed that the people did not practice justice and that they did not cry out to God for justice.

In the last chapter, we discussed the fact that God calls us to pray for our leaders. By implication, then, we are also called to pray for justice. For it is when leaders practice justice that God will bring about good things in our country.

THE DARE

Today I want you to pray for justice. Maybe you feel like you are the subject of injustice in your life in some way. I also want you to look beyond yourself and pray for justice in your city, state and country. Wherever you see injustice, pray for justice. God loves justice, so this is a powerful prayer, for you are praying for something that is in His will.

What are some of the injustices you see in your city, your state and your country?

_____

_____

_____

_____

_____

What are some ways that you are praying for justice today?

_____

_____

_____

_____

_____

Do you have any answers to prayer from yesterday or the day before? List them here.

_____

_____

_____

_____

_____

Note

1. Michela Wrong, *It's Our Turn to Eat: The Story of a Kenyan Whistle-Blower* (New York: HarperCollins Publishers, 2009), pp. 77-78.

38

Pray for Healing

*Is any one of you sick? He should call the elders of the church to
pray over him and anoint him with oil in the name of the Lord.
And the prayer offered in faith will make the sick person well.*
JAMES 5:14-15

Mutemi Mwinzi was a very sick man. A member of a church in
Kenya in 1963, he was stricken by a strange illness that none of
the doctors seemed able to treat or relieve. Though he prayed,
took medication and even consulted a witch doctor, he resigned
himself to the sad truth that he probably had a terminal illness
and would soon die. People abandoned him. Family and friends
refused to care for him. Visitors came by each day to see him
but only stopped by to see if he had died.

Mutemi, who knew a few verses in the Bible, remembered
Psalm 27:10: "My father and my mother have forsaken me, but
the LORD will take me up" (*NASB*). He quoted the verse over and
over and cried out repeatedly to God for help. When he figured
there was no more hope, he dragged himself outside to die.
About 10 yards from his hut, he pleaded with God one more
time to either heal him or let him die. He promised the Lord
that if he were healed, he would spend the rest of his life serving Him and would give all that he had to the church.

As Mutemi whispered his resolve to the Lord, his body began to shiver. Within moments he crumpled to the ground in

convulsions. He drifted into unconsciousness. When he awakened, the sickness was gone—completely. For the first time in days he felt hungry. He walked back into his small house to find something to eat. Sometime later, when his family and friends found him eating at the table, he explained to them everything that had happened.

The following Sunday, Mutemi told his story to a church filled with people. Many of those who had never been in church before went forward to receive Christ. The church experienced instant revival. Mutemi, who was a wealthy man by village standards, promised to take responsibility for the pastor's salary and to build a new church. Men and women came from around the country to hear his story. Within a year, the church membership grew from 50 to 300 people.[1]

Mutemi's experience with praying for healing stands in stark contrast to C. S. Lewis's experience when prayers offered to God for the healing of his wife went unanswered (see chapter 27). One person was healed; one, not. Both trusted in Christ; but only one was made well, and one died. What are we to believe about healing when people have such divergent experiences? Unfortunately, many Christians move to one of two extremes.

At one pole are those who neither expect nor pray for miracles of healing. At the other pole are Christians who pursue healing with such zeal that it becomes the primary focus of their faith. They expect God to heal every sniffle or scratch, and they report marvelous accounts of healing. One person said of such zealous Christians, "Those excited about healing tell the truth, the whole truth, and a little more than the truth." They tend to exaggerate, and they skip telling about the nonhealings. So what are we to believe about healing?

James, one of the leaders of the Early Church, tells us to ask for healing: "Is any one of you sick? He should call the elders of the church to pray over him and anoint him with oil in the name of the Lord. And the prayer offered in faith will make the sick person well" (Jas. 5:14-15). It is always right for us to pray for healing. Jesus healed, the apostles healed, and God still heals today.

Years ago, in obedience to God's instructions in James, we at Sunset Presbyterian started offering prayers for healing in our worship services. Not all people who have asked for healing have been healed, but many have. One woman wrote to me about her experience:

Dear Pastor Ron,

In the past two years I have attended two healing services for my mother who has twice attempted suicide. She has a long history of mental and emotional problems. For over a year she lived at a residential care center. Today, thanks to your healing services, she is at home with my dad again. She is functionally well and going for marriage counseling with my dad. Although I kept my mom in prayer daily, the healing service provided me with another important way of petitioning God on my mother's behalf. Over a year ago I was afraid that my mom would never be well enough to come home. Thank you, Ron, for the healing services at Sunset. The healing prayers were so powerful.

Obviously, God does answer prayer to heal someone who is sick.

On the other hand, God did not promise to heal every time we ask. The apostle Paul asked God to heal him, but God said no (see chapter 27). We make a mistake when we think God must heal us or those we pray for every time we ask for healing. God doesn't heal everyone. Sometimes God receives more glory through a sickness or death.

So it is always right to ask for healing. In fact, most people should pray for healing more often than they do. If you are not in the habit of asking God to heal yourself and the people you love, I encourage you to do so. I also encourage you to contact your pastor or the leaders in your church and ask them to pray for you in obedience to God's command in James. Every time someone in our family is sick or struggling with some injury, I pray for healing. Every time someone comes to me at church with some sickness, I pray for the person before he or she leaves my office. But don't demand that God heal. And don't think something is wrong with God or your faith if God does not immediately answer your prayer or does not answer the way you wanted or expected Him to. Have the humility to admit that you don't always know what God's will is and what will bring Him the most glory.

THE DARE

Today I want you to pray for healing. What physical or emotional struggles do you face? Ask God to heal you. Ask Him to be gracious toward you. Go to your pastor or the leaders in your church and ask them to pray for you in obedience to God's command in the book of James. If friends or family members are dealing with health issues, ask if you can pray for them as well. Ask boldly for God to heal, but also ask humbly, recognizing that it may not be God's will to heal at this time.

Who are the people and what are the ailments you asked God to heal today?

_____

_____

_____

_____

_____

What answers to your prayers for healing (or any other answers to prayer) have you received recently?

_____

_____

_____

_____

_____

Note

1. Ron Kincaid, *Praying for Guidance: How to Discover God's Will* (Downers Grove, IL: InterVarsity, 1996), pp. 122-123.

39

Pray in Response to God's Promptings

Do not put out the Spirit's fire.
1 THESSALONIANS 5:19

Prayer is a two-way process. Throughout this book, I have talked about how we talk to God in prayer. But prayer also involves listening to God. Some of the most important things for us to listen to as followers of Christ are God's promptings. Every day I receive promptings from the Holy Spirit—I sense God, through His still, small voice, urging me to do something or not do something. One time I was urged to show special sensitivity and kindness to my wife. Another time I was told to slow down and help one of my children with something. One time I was prompted to call my mom. More than once I've been warned to take a deep breath and not lose my temper. Another time I received a strong sense that I ought to stop and talk to a staff member at church. One time I sensed that I should stop and speak to a stranger I was passing on the street. Many times I've gotten a sense that I need to stop and pray for someone. Whatever the prompting is, I have learned not to ignore it, because it comes from the Holy Spirit.

God works through people who commit their lives to Him, people who are filled with the Holy Spirit. And we connect ourselves to the power of the Holy Spirit through prayer, both talking to Him and listening to Him.

A few months ago I came downstairs into the kitchen, because I wanted to use the microwave, but the kids told me the microwave did not work. And sure enough, it didn't work. So I walked downstairs to the electrical panel, where I saw that the switch for the microwave was tripped. I flipped it back, and the microwave worked fine.

We're like that microwave: Without prayer, the power switch has been turned off in our lives. Prayer is how we connect to the power. Listening for the promptings of the Holy Spirit connects us to His power throughout the day.

And one of the ways God takes care of His children who are in need is to prompt other followers to pray for them.

An American soldier serving in Vietnam had come to the end of his tour of duty and was looking forward to going home. The much-anticipated day to return home arrived, and his commander said to him, "I want you to go on one last mission." So he went out into the jungle to look for the unseen enemy. He felt confident because he had gone on so many missions, he knew exactly where all the mines were—except one. He stepped on the mine and suddenly found himself dangling upside down in a trap. Having lost his weapon, he watched as a Viet Cong soldier approached him with a bayonet in his hand, ready to pierce him in the heart. Suddenly the soldier's whole life flashed before him. He knew that unless God did something fast, he had come to the moment of his death. So he prayed that God might deliver him. Then just as suddenly as the Viet Cong soldier appeared, he laid down his weapon and walked away.

Three and a half years later, the veteran shared his amazing story of God delivering him in the jungle in a talk he gave to a group of people that included an elderly woman who approached him after he was done speaking. She told him that three and a half years earlier, she was praying for the service-men and servicewomen in Vietnam, when God enabled her to see this very same young man on his final mission and the whole sequence of events as he had just described. As she saw the events unfold, she cried out for God to deliver and rescue the young man. She was so excited now, because until she heard his speech, she hadn't known how God had dramatically an-swered her prayer.

God enabled her to see this young man in danger, prompted her to pray for him, and she did. Without a doubt, that young soldier is grateful that she had listened to the prompting of the Holy Spirit.

Paul said, "Do not put out the Spirit's fire" (1 Thess. 5:19). We are not to quench or ignore the Spirit's promptings. Instead, we are to respond to them.

Many times when I have been worried about one of the members of my family, I have felt a prompting from God to pray for him or her. It's almost inevitable that I later learn that, sure enough, the person had been facing a really difficult chal-lenge at that moment. It's important that when I get this sense from God that I should pray for someone, I pray.

Often when I get a prompting to pray for someone, I don't know exactly what to pray. Then I seek guidance from God as to how I should pray: "The Spirit helps us in our weakness. We do not know what we ought to pray for, but the Spirit himself intercedes for us with groans that words cannot express" (Rom. 8:26). Paul didn't say *you* don't know how to pray. He said *we* don't know how to pray. Even *he* didn't know how to pray at times. That's when we seek guidance from God.

Listen for the Spirit's promptings throughout the day, and do what He says.

THE DARE

Today as you go through your day, look for and listen for the Spirit's promptings. If you slow down and listen for the Holy Spirit's promptings, you will find that He speaks to you many times each day. Maybe He will urge you to say something kind and encouraging to someone. Maybe you will get a sense that you should do something for someone. It could be a prompting to pray for someone. Whatever it is, tell God that you covenant to do it.

What promptings did you feel you received from the Holy Spirit?

_____

_____

_____

_____

_____

What did you do in response to the Spirit's promptings? What resulted from any action you took?

_____

_____

_____

_____

_____

40

Putting It All Together

We've been at this together for 40 days. For 40 days we've prayed. For 40 days we've considered different aspects of prayer. I hope you've enjoyed the journey. Let's look back for a moment at some of the high points of where we've been.

First, we discovered the importance of knowing to whom we pray. We pray to a God who loves us. We pray to a God who is gracious. We pray to a God who is willing. We pray to a God who only gives good gifts. Reminding ourselves that we pray to a Father in heaven who loves us dearly draws us to prayer. Why wouldn't we want to pray to a God who loves us as much as He does?

Another thing we learned is the simple fact that prayer is important. Prayer is the primary way God has ordained for us to communicate with Him. Jesus prayed constantly. If He felt the need to pray, how much more must we? There are many struggles we face in life that can only be overcome by prayer. If we are going to discover an intimate relationship with God and the power in prayer, we have to pray. We need to pray about everything.

Just this week, I had an experience that shows the amazing power of prayer and the importance of praying about everything. I came out of the grocery store, and as I headed for my car, the wind blew something into my eye. Since I wear contacts, it hurt immediately. Even though it was very uncomfortable,

I figured that if I blinked my eye enough, my tears would wash away the speck from my eye. That didn't work. One mile down the road, I stopped my car and walked into another store to check my contact in a restroom mirror. Even though the light was not good (the light over the sink was burned out), I took my contact out, rinsed it off, and put it back.

As I walked from the restroom, I looked through my reinserted contact to check my vision. It was blurry. I thought that was odd. How could I have smudged it that badly? So I returned to the bathroom to check my contact. Through the dim lighting, I looked for the contact in my eye. I couldn't find it. I thought I felt it somewhere in my eye, so I looked all around my eye, but still I couldn't locate it. I looked to see if I had dropped it in the sink. There was nothing.

Suddenly, I felt a sense of desperation. These were brand-new contacts. Where was it? For a moment, I thought I would drive home and look for it in my eye under better light. Suddenly I prayed, "Lord, please help me find it." At that instant, I whirled around and looked on the bathroom floor, which several men had walked over while I was there. There in the middle of the floor—right where those other men had walked—lay my contact. I couldn't believe it. It could easily have been smashed, but it lay there intact.

God had protected it. God had directed me to look for it there in the store rather than heading home. God had showed it to me on the floor of a busy public restroom. God was gracious, but first I had to ask for His help. I doubt if I would have found it if I had not asked for His divine guidance. We have to pray if we want to experience God's power in our lives.

This leads to another thing we learned on our journey: We must begin our prayers with praise. We praise God for who He

is. We praise God for His greatness. We praise Him for His power. We praise Him that He is omnipotent. We praise Him that He is omniscient. We praise Him for His love and grace and forgiveness. Praise reminds us that God cares about us and our problems. Praise reminds us that God is greater than our troubles. There is no difficulty too great for Him. Praise takes our minds off of our struggles and lifts them to God. Praise changes our perspective. Praise releases the power of God in our lives. We cannot praise God too much, and we cannot overemphasize the importance of praise.

We also looked at the importance of confession in prayer. We must ask forgiveness for our sins. We must admit how often we fail to do what God asks of us and commit ourselves to obeying God's commands. We can hardly expect God to take our requests seriously if we do not take His requests seriously. Because we disobey God's commands so frequently, obviously we must come to God humbly. We cannot come to prayer with the attitude that God owes us something. We dare not come thinking that after all we've done for God, He had better do something big for us. Instead, we come humbly, recognizing that God doesn't owe us anything. We don't deserve anything.

From his earliest days, our third son had a love for horses. So, for his eleventh birthday, we bought him a horse. Over the years, our son has acquired other horses and bred them, and we have had numerous horses on our property. Our son has taken full responsibility for caring for them. The rest of us do not know much about horses.

One day, the horses got out of our fence and were walking down the street. I think we had four horses at the time. Jorie yelled, "The horses are out. Help!" All of us who were home were suddenly on horse duty. Jorie and I and the three or four kids who were home joined us outside. The problem was that our son who takes care of the horses was not home. We called him, but it would take him nearly a half hour to get home. So the rest of us went outside to try to restore order and get the horses back in the fence. Jorie gave us all apples to hold in our hands. We thought the apples might lure them back inside the fence, but they didn't. So we fanned out around our property in an attempt to herd them back through the gate. That didn't work either. I started feeling a little silly and seriously helpless. Here I was a grown man, and I couldn't corral the horses.

Finally, our son got home. He gave a couple tongue clicks, and all the horses trotted to him and rushed through the gate. I couldn't believe it.

"How did you do that?" I asked incredulously.

He said, "In every pack of horses, there is an alpha horse. The alpha horse is in charge. When the alpha horse wants water, he goes straight to the water, and the other horses get out of the way. If you want to lead horses, you have to become the alpha horse. If you're not in charge and aren't confident, they can sense it and won't come to you." It was a humbling experience to have my son do in one minute what I couldn't do in 30 minutes. When we come to God in prayer, we must come humbly.

Still another important thing we learned during our 40-day journey in prayer is that our prayers are more effective when we ask for things that are in God's will. One of the best ways to figure out if our requests are in God's will is to determine if what we are requesting will bring Him glory. When we ask for things that will bring honor to God, more than likely we are asking for things that are in His will. Only when we are absolutely certain that what we are asking of God is in His will can we pray with faith that we will receive what we ask. When we are reasonably confident that we are asking God for things that will bring credit to Him, then it is important that we pray with resolute faith.

We also learned that we must always be totally honest with God. If we want to develop intimacy with God through prayer, we have to start with transparency. We need to tell God how we are feeling, including our fears and worries, our loneliness, our disappointments, even our upsets that He didn't answer our prayers. God can handle all of our problems. In the process of being really honest with God about our feelings, we draw closer to Him, and we are much more likely to learn that we can trust that He will take care of us.

I hope you have developed a new pattern of prayer in your life. I trust you have learned to tell God everything you are thinking and to pray about everything. I hope you have learned how much God loves you and wants to meet your needs.

These are some of the high points we encountered along the way. However, perhaps the most important lesson we learned is that we just need to get alone with God daily and pray. If you've prayed with me for 40 days and written down answers to prayer, hopefully you have developed a new pattern of prayer in your life. Hopefully you have learned to pray on a daily basis. I trust that you have learned to tell God everything you are thinking and to pray about everything. I hope that you have learned how much God loves you and how much He wants to meet your needs. I'm guessing that you've also learned to begin your prayers with praise and that you've learned to confess your sins and come to God in an attitude of humility. And I do hope that you are learning to pray for things that are in God's will that bring God glory.

Lament, desire, need, praise, confession, humility, honesty, persistence, confidence, obedience, cooperation, faith, passion, desperation, trust, fasting—God wants to hear and see it all in prayer. So I dare you to pray!

THE DARE

Today, as you finish the prayer dare, I want you to write out the important things you learned from this journey. What are the most important lessons you learned that you never want to forget?

_____

_____

_____

_____

_____

What were some of the most amazing answers to prayer you received during this 40-day journey? List them below.

_____

_____

_____

_____

_____

You can contact Ron Kincaid at
ronkincaid@sterlink.net